HTML5 MOBILE
Pocket Primer

LICENSE, DISCLAIMER OF LIABILITY, AND LIMITED WARRANTY

HTML5 MOBILE
for Android and iOS
Pocket Primer

Oswald Campesato

MERCURY LEARNING AND INFORMATION
Dulles, Virginia
Boston, Massachusetts
New Delhi

Publisher: David Pallai
Mercury Learning and Information
22841 Quicksilver Drive
Dulles, VA 20166
info@merclearning.com
www.merclearning.com
1-800-758-3756

O. Campesato. *HTML5 Mobile for Android and iOS Pocket Primer.*
ISBN: 978-1-938549-66-3

Library of Congress Control Number: 2013952878

131415321   Printed in the United States of America
This book is printed on acid-free paper.

I'd like to dedicate this book to my parents –
may this bring joy and happiness into their lives.

CONTENTS

PREFACE

WHAT IS THE PRIMARY VALUE PROPOSITION FOR THIS BOOK?

This book endeavors to provide you with as much up-to-date information as possible regarding HTML5 hybrid mobile applications that can be reasonably included in a book of this size. There are several significant features of this book, including a CSS3 chapter that covers CSS3 2D/3D graphics and animation, an SVG Appendix (with custom code samples), and an appendix for HTML5 `Canvas`. This book contains an additional appendix that is devoted to D3, which can be used in HTML5 hybrid applications.

Finally, there are numerous open source projects (links are provided toward the end of this Preface) containing code samples so that you can explore the capabilities of CSS3, SVG, HTML5 `Canvas`, and jQuery combined with CSS3.

THE TARGET AUDIENCE

This book is intended to reach an international audience of readers with highly diverse backgrounds and various age groups. While many readers know how to read English, their native spoken language is not English (which could be their second, third, or even fourth language). Consequently, this book uses standard English rather than colloquial expressions that might be confusing to those readers. As you know, many people learn by different types of mimicry, which includes reading, writing, or hearing new material. This book takes these points into consideration in order to provide a comfortable and meaningful learning experience for the intended readers.

GETTING THE MOST FROM THIS BOOK

Some programmers learn well from prose, others learn well from sample code (and lots of it), which means that there's no single style works perfectly for everyone.

Moreover, some programmers want to run the code first, see what it does, and then return to the code to understand the details (and others use the opposite approach).

Consequently, there is a variety of code samples in this book. Some are short, some are long, and other code samples "build" from earlier code samples.

The goal is to show (and not just tell) you a variety of visual effects that are possible, some of which you might not find anywhere else. You benefit from this approach because you can pick and choose the visual effects and the code that creates those visual effects.

HOW WAS THE CODE FOR THIS BOOK TESTED?

The code samples in this book have been tested in a Google Chrome browser (version 26.0.1500.95) on a Macbook Pro with OS X 10.8.2. The HTML5 hybrid applications were deployed to a Nexus 7 2 with JellyBean 4.3, an Asus Prime 10" tablet with Android ICS, and a Sprint 4G S with Android ICS. Also keep in mind is that all references to "Web Inspector" refer to the Web Inspector in Chrome, which differs from the Web Inspector in Safari. If you are using a different (but still modern) browser or an early version of Chrome, you might need to check online for the sequence of keystrokes that you need to follow to launch and view the Web Inspector. Navigate to this link for additional useful information:

http://benalman.com/projects/javascript-debug-console-log/

WHAT DO I NEED TO KNOW FOR THIS BOOK?

The most important prerequisite is familiarity with HTML Web pages and some familiarity with CSS3 and JavaScript. If you want to be sure that you can grasp the material in this book, glance through some of the code samples to get an idea of how much is familiar to you and how much is new for you.

WHY DOES THIS BOOK HAVE 200 PAGES INSTEAD OF 500 PAGES?

This book is part of a Pocket Primer series whose books are between 200 and 250 pages. Second, the target audience consists of readers ranging from beginners to intermediate in terms of their knowledge of HTML, CSS3, and JavaScript. During the preparation of this book, every effort has been made to accommodate those readers so that they will be adequately prepared to explore more advanced features of these technologies during their self study.

DOESN'T THE DVD OBVIATE THE NEED FOR THIS BOOK?

The DVD contains all the code samples to save you time and effort from the error-prone process of manually typing code into an HTML Web page. In addition, there are situations in which you might not have easy access to DVD. Furthermore, the code samples in the book provide explanations that are not available on the DVD.

Finally, as mentioned earlier in this Preface, there are some introductory videos available that cover HTML5, CSS3, HTML5 `Canvas`, and SVG. Navigate to the publisher's Website to obtain more information regarding their availability.

DOES THIS BOOK CONTAIN PRODUCTION-LEVEL CODE SAMPLES?

The primary purpose of the code samples in this book is to illustrate various features HTML5, CSS3, and JavaScript that you can use in order to create HTML5 hybrid mobile applications. Clarity has higher priority than writing more compact code that is more difficult to understand (and possibly more prone to bugs). If you decide to use any of the code in this book in a production Website, you ought to subject that code to the same rigorous analysis as the other parts of your HTML Web pages.

OTHER RELATED BOOKS BY THE AUTHOR

1) HTML5 Canvas and CSS3:

http://www.amazon.com/HTML5-Canvas-CSS3-Graphics-Primer/ dp/1936420341

2) jQuery, HTML5, and CSS3:

http://www.amazon.com/jQuery-HTML5-Mobile-Desktop-Devices/ dp/1938549031

3) HTML5 Pocket Primer:

http://www.amazon.com/HTML5-Pocket-Primer-Oswald-Campesato/ dp/1938549104

4) jQuery Pocket Primer:

http://www.amazon.com/dp/1938549147

Upcoming books by the author include:
5) HTML5 Canvas Pocket Primer
6) CSS3 Pocket Primer

The following open source projects contain code samples that supplement the material in various chapters of this book:

https://code.google.com/p/css3-graphics/

https://code.google.com/p/d3-graphics/
https://code.google.com/p/html5-canvas-graphics/
https://code.google.com/p/jquery-css3-graphics/
https://code.google.com/p/raphael-graphics/
https://code.google.com/p/svg-filters-graphics/
https://code.google.com/p/svg-graphics/

O.C
Menlo Park, CA

ABOUT THE TECHNICAL EDITOR

Richard Clark, M.A. (@rdclark) is an experienced software developer and instructor for Kaazing Corporation. He has taught for Apple and Hewlett-Packard, written immersive simulations, developed multiple high-performance web applications for the Fortune 100, and published Apple iOS applications. An in-demand speaker for international conferences, he has a special interest in using mobile, connected, real-time applications to help people live, work, and play better. In his spare time, Richard does web development for non-profits, tends a garden full of California native plants, and cooks for family and charity events.

## CHAPTER 1

HTML5 AND MOBILE

In this chapter, you will learn about the W3C and the WHATWG, and also about HTML5-specific elements for semantic markup. You will also learn about some Websites that provide very useful information, such as browser support for HTML5 features. If you are new to HTML5, keep in mind that some of its features can vary considerably in terms of the complexity of their associated APIs. Fortunately, you can find jQuery plugins (and other tools) that provide a layer of abstraction over some of the more complex HTML5 APIs. Consequently, it's to your advantage to be aware of tools that can simplify your HTML5-related development.

WHAT IS HTML5?

HTML5 currently consists of a mixture of technologies, some of which are formally included in the HTML5 specification, and some which are not part of the specification. There are few people who seem to know the "definition" of HTML5, and perhaps that's why Peter Paul Koch (creator of the quirksmode Website) wryly suggested that "whatever Web technology you're working on that's cool right now. . .that's HTML5." As you will discover, HTML5 means different things to different people, so don't be surprised if you cannot get one consistent "definition" of HTML5 (if only the situation were so simple!).

HTML5 is the latest version of HTML that is backward compatible with most features of earlier versions of HTML. In addition to its plugin-free architecture, HTML5 provides a wealth of new features: new tags for audio, video, semantic markup; new input types and validation for forms; local and session storage; support for graphics-based APIs in Canvas; and communication-related techniques such as server sent events and Web sockets.

Although CSS3 is not a formal part of HTML5, many people consider it to be an important part of HTML5 Web pages. As you will see in Chapter 3, CSS3 provides support for rich visual effects, including 2D/3D graphics and animation.

With regard to HTML, you have probably seen many Web pages with HTML that rely on a combination of HTML `<table>` elements and HTML `<div>` elements. Such tags are generic, and it can be difficult to determine what role each one plays in the finished page. The good news is that the new HTML5 semantic tags provide more meaningful information about the purpose of each section in an HTML5 Web page, which can be discerned much more easily than Web pages written in HTML4. You will see an example of using some of these semantic tags later in this chapter.

One of the exciting aspects of HTML5 is that it's designed to run on desktop devices as well as mobile devices. In fact, HTML5-based mobile applications offer speed of development and deployment to multiple mobile devices with one code base, which is appealing to developers of mobile applications that do not require intensive computations (such as games) or access to hardware features (such as accelerometer).

Although you can use PhoneGap to perform push notifications, Web-based mobile applications do not support Android-specific features such as adding ringtones or changing the wallpaper (which are typically user features). On the other hand, you can transfer files using the regular AJAX API (`XmlHT-TPRequest`), and File APIs are supported on Android (via JavaScript), with upcoming iOS support:

http://caniuse.com/#feat=fileapi.

There is one other point to keep in mind: the specification for HTML 4.01 (the predecessor to HTML5) was introduced in 1999, so HTML5 represents the largest advance in HTML in 10 years, and perhaps the inclusion of other technologies was inevitable. There is a great deal of excitement surrounding HTML5, and a major update regarding the specification is scheduled for 2014. Indeed, the enthusiasm for HTML5 may have accelerated the speed with which HTML5 will become a formal specification based on open standards.

Browser Support for HTML5

The WebKit-based browsers (Chrome and Safari), as well as Mozilla Firefox, Opera, and IE10 support many HTML5 features, on desktops as well as mobile devices. In addition to the well-known browsers, there are browsers such as the Dolphin browser and the browser provided by the Tizen OS, and in mid-2012, they were the top-ranked browsers in terms of support for HTML5 features. In 2013, Google announced the availability of Blink, which is a new rendering engine for Google Chrome. Blink is a fork of WebKit, and according to Google, this new code base will result in simpler code and faster release cycles. You can read more details from various people here:

http://www.quirksmode.org/blog/archives/2013/04/blink.html.

As you know, this book focuses on WebKit-based browsers, and all code samples have been tested on a Chrome browser on a Macbook. In addition, virtually every code sample in this book can be deployed on at least one of the following devices:

- an Asus Prime tablet with Android Ice Cream Sandwich
- a Nexus 7.2 with Android JellyBean (Android 4.3)
- an iPad running on iOS 5
- a Sprint Nexus S 4G with Android ICS (or higher)

The only exceptions are the code samples (and associated screenshots) in Chapter 4 that illustrate the most recent features of CSS3 (such as CSS Shaders) that are rendered in a special Chromium build from Adobe running on a Macbook. The download link for this special build is in Chapter 3, and you can expect these new CSS3 features to be supported in the near future. In fact, work is already underway on CSS Blending and Compositing:

http://www.webkit.org/blog/2102/last-week-in-webkit-a-new-content-security-policy-api-and-transitioning-from-percentages-to-pixels.

HTML5 AND VARIOUS WORKING GROUPS

The *W3C* (World Wide Web Consortium), the *WHATWG* (Web Hypertext Application Technology Working Group), and the *DAP* (Device APIs Working Group) are organizations that provide the specifications and APIs for HTML5 and mobile devices that are covered in this book. In addition, the IETF (Internet Engineering Task Force) handles the networking standards (such as WebSockets, SPDY, CORS, and so forth), but not the actual APIs, and its homepage is here:

https://www.ietf.org/.

The W3C is an international community for various groups to work together to develop Web standards. The W3C is led by Web inventor Tim Berners-Lee and CEO, Jeffrey Jaffe, and its homepage is here:

http://www.w3.org.

Every proposal submitted to the W3C undergoes the following sequence in order to become a W3C Recommendation:

- Working Draft (WD)
- Candidate Recommendation (CR)
- Proposed Recommendation (PR)
- W3C Recommendation (REC)
- Later revisions

The HTML5-related technologies that have been submitted to the W3C are in different stages of the W3C "evaluation" process. The following link contains a diagram that provides a succinct visual display of HTML5 technologies and their status in December, 2011:

http://en.wikipedia.org/wiki/File:HTML5-APIs-and-related-technologies-by-Sergey-Mavrody.png.

If you want to find the most recent status updates, the following link provides a list of HTML5 APIs and their status:

http://www.w3.org/TR/.

Click on the link "JavaScript APIs" in the preceding Website, or simply navigate to this URL which shows you the most recent status of HTML5 APIs:

http://www.w3.org/TR/#tr_Javascript_APIs.

The WHATWG focuses primarily on the development of HTML and APIs needed for Web applications. The WHATWG was founded in 2004 by employees of Apple, the Mozilla Foundation, and Opera Software. The main focus of the WHATWG is the HTML standard, which also includes Web Workers, Web Storage, the Web Sockets API, and Server-Sent Events. The following are two links with additional information about the WHATWG:

http://www.whatwg.org/ and *http://wiki.whatwg.org/wiki/FAQ.*

HTML5 is a joint effort involving the W3C (World Wide Web Consortium) and the WHATWG (Web Hypertext Application Technology Working Group). If you enjoy reading proposals, you will find links for various W3C Specifications, mainly in this chapter and Chapter 10.

Another group is the Device APIs Working Group, whose mission is to create client-side APIs that enable the development of Web Applications and Web Widgets that interact with devices services such as Calendar, Contacts, Camera, and so forth. Currently, the DAP is actively working on the following specifications:

- Battery Status API
- HTML Media Capture
- Media Capture and Streams
- Network Information API
- Proximity Events
- Vibration API
- Web Intents (service discovery)

Additional information about the status of these (and other) DAP specifications is here:

http://www.w3.org/2009/dap/.

HTML5 SPECIFICATIONS: W3C OR WHATWG?

In essence, the WHATWG has the master specification, which the W3C HTML Working Group takes as the foundation for the "official" specification.

The W3C synchronizes its work with the WHATWG, mostly reformatting to match its publication style (including breaking it into sub-specifications).

The exact list of changes in the introduction to the WHATWG form of the specification is here:

http://www.whatwg.org/specs/web-apps/current-work/multipage/ introduction.html#introduction.

Now that you know a little bit about the groups that are in charge of various specifications, let's explore some of the facets of HTML5.

WHAT TECHNOLOGIES ARE INCLUDED IN HTML5?

The following list contains a combination of technologies that are formally included in the HTML5 specification, as well as several other technologies that are frequently associated with HTML5:

- Canvas 2D
- CSS3
- Drag-and-Drop (DnD)
- File API
- Geolocation
- Microdata
- Offline Applications
- Server-Sent Events (SSE)
- SVG
- Web Intents
- Web Messaging
- Web Sockets
- Web Storage
- Web Workers

There are other technologies that are often associated with HTML5, including WebGL and XHR2 (XmlHTTPRequest Level 2).

Incidentally, the following link contains a diagram that provides a succinct visual display of HTML5 technologies and their status in December, 2011:

http://en.wikipedia.org/wiki/File:HTML5-APIs-and-related-technologies- by-Sergey-Mavrody.png.

The preceding link classifies HTML5 technologies as follows:

- W3C Recommendation
- Candidate Recommendation
- Last Call
- Working Draft
- Non-W3C Specification
- Deprecated W3C APIs

Keep in mind that the status of some of these technologies will change, so be sure to visit the link with the details of the W3C specification for each of these technologies in order to find their most recent status. If you plan to use jQuery in your HTML5 Web pages, it's worth looking for the availability of jQuery plugins for many of the HTML5 technologies in the preceding diagram.

DIFFERENCES BETWEEN HTML4 TAGS AND HTML5 TAGS

Broadly speaking, HTML5 differs from earlier versions of HTML in the following ways:

- some HTML4.x elements are no longer supported
- HTML5 provides support for new elements
- HTML5 simplifies some existing elements
- HTML5 provides support for custom attributes

Some new tags in HTML5: `<article>`, `<aside>`, `<audio>`, `<canvas>`, `<command>`, `<datalist>`, `<details>`, `<dialog>`, `<figure>`, `<footer>`, `<header>`, `<keygen>`, `<mark>`, `<meter>`, `<nav>`, `<output>`, `<progress>`, `<rp>`, `<rt>`, `<ruby>`, `<section>`, `<source>`, `<time>`, and `<video>`.

The HTML elements that are not recommended for new work in HTML5 (many of which have been replaced with CSS styling) include the following: `<acronym>`, `<applet>`, `<basefont>`, `<big>`, `<center>`, `<dir>`, `<font>`, `<frame>`, `<frameset>`, `<noframes>`, `<s>`, `<strike>`, `<tt>`, and `<u>`.

You are probably already aware of the new HTML5 `<audio>` tag and HTML5 `<video>` tag, and later in this chapter, you'll see examples of how to use these tags in HTML5 Web pages.

One important new HTML5 feature is support for custom data attributes, which always have a `data-` prefix. This support for custom data attributes provides HTML5 markup with some of the functionality that is available in XML, which enables code to process custom tags and their values and also pass validation at the same time. In fact, jQuery Mobile makes *very* extensive use of custom data attributes, and you will see an example later in this chapter.

If you want additional details, a full list of the differences between HTML5 and HTML4 is in this W3C document:

http://dev.w3.org/html5/html4-differences/

USEFUL ONLINE TOOLS FOR HTML5 DEVELOPMENT

Before delving into the new HTML5 tags that are discussed in this chapter, you need to know about the online tools that can assist in creating well-designed HTML5 Web pages. These tools are available because of one important fact: modern browsers differ in terms of their support for HTML5 features (for desktop browsers and also for mobile browsers). Fortunately, tools such as

`Modernizr` enable you to detect HTML5 feature support in modern browsers using simple JavaScript code.

Modernizr

`Modernizr` is a very useful tool for HTML5-related feature detection in various browsers, and its homepage is here:

http://www.modernizr.com/

In case you didn't already know, server-side "browser sniffing" used to be a popular technique for detecting the browser that you were using to render a particular Web page, but this technique is not as accurate (or as "clean") due to rapidly changing implementations in browsers. Indeed, the most popular Websites that check for HTML5 support use feature detection and not browser sniffing. For example, Safari on the iPad has used the following user agent string:

```
Mozilla/5.0 (iPad; U; CPU OS 3_2_1 like Mac OS X; en-us)
AppleWebKit/531.21.10 (KHTML, like Gecko) Mobile/7B405
```

At some point you will start using JavaScript in your HTML5 Web pages (indeed, you probably do so already), and `Modernizr` provides a programmatic way to check for many HTML5 and CSS3 features in different browsers.

In order to use `Modernizr`, include the following code snippet in the `<head>` element of your Web pages:

```
<script src="modernizr.min.js" type="text/javascript"></script>
```

The following type of code block illustrates one way that you can use `Modernizr` in an HTML page:

```
if(Modernizr.canvas) {
  // canvas is available
  // do something here
} else {
  // canvas is not available
  // do something else here
}
```

Note: Unlike many scripts that can be inserted after the body of the page, `Modernizr` is designed to run *before* the page is rendered and before any other scripts.

Navigate to the `Modernizr` homepage where you can read the documentation, tutorials, and details regarding the set of feature detection.

Caniuse

The following Website ("When Can I Use. . .") is extremely useful because it provides information regarding support for many HTML5 features in modern browsers:

http://www.caniuse.com

Currently, there are two main tabs on this Website. The first (and default) tab is divided into a number of sections (CSS, HTML5, SVG, JS API, and Other), and each section contains a list of technical items that are hyperlinks to other Web pages that provide detailed information.

The second tab on this Website is called "tables," and when you click on this tab, you will see a tabular display of information in a set of tables. The columns in each table are modern browsers, and the rows specify features, and the cells in the tables provide the browser version numbers where the specified features are supported.

The following Website also provides very useful information regarding HTML5:

http://html5boilerplate.com/

USING FEATURE DETECTION IN HTML WEB PAGES

Browser, or UA sniffing, refers to parsing the User Agent string available in every browser, and then using the results to determine how to proceed. However, browser sniffing is unreliable and it's been replaced by feature detection, which checks for the availability of features in a browser. Feature detection can treat new browsers in the same manner as current browsers, whereas browser sniffing uses hard-coded strings (which might also contain regular expressions), so new code must be added whenever a new browser becomes available.

The four basic ways to detect for HTML5 functions are listed here:

- Check for the property on a global object
- Check for the property on an element you create
- Check that a method returns a correct value
- Check that an element retains a value

Every HTML5 document is displayed in a global element, which is usually called the navigator or the window. You can use a global element to test whether or not offline Web applications are supported in a browser as shown here:

```
if(window.applicationCache) {
    console.logwrite("Your browser supports offline apps.");
} else {
    console.log("Your browser does not support offline web apps.");
}
```

If your browser supports the `applicationCache` item, then it can use features such as online/offline detection, the offline application cache, and so forth.

An example of testing whether or not an element retains a value is shown here:

```
var div = document.createElement('div');
div.style.cssText = "background-color:rgba(150,255,150,.5)";
```

```
if(!!~('' + div.style.backgroundColor).indexOf('rgba')){
// rgba is supported so do something here
}
```

The ! ! in the preceding code snippet guarantees that its enclosed expression is converted to a Boolean value, and conveniently handles the case in which a variable is undefined. An even simpler way to check for feature support is illustrated in the following JavaScript code block that defines three global Boolean variables:

```
var supportsLocation = !!navigator.geolocation;
var supportsStorage  = !!window.localStorage;
var supportsVideo    = !!document.createElement("video").
canPlayType;
```

`Modernizr` uses feature detection and is well-suited for handling a vast array of feature-related checks. However, if you want to use JavaScript to detect support for CSS3 features in a browser, the following link contains a clever way to check for feature support in multiple browsers (so it uses vendor-specific features):

http://net.tutsplus.com/tutorials/html-css-techniques/quick-tip-detect-css-support-in-browsers-with-javascript/

A SIMPLE HTML5 WEB PAGE

In addition to introducing many new semantic tags, HTML5 has simplified several tags, including the <DOCTYPE> declaration and the attributes `lang` and `charset`. Listing 1.1 displays `Sample1.html`, which is an HTML5 Web page that illustrates the simplified syntax of HTML5.

Note: This code sample illustrates the structure of a simple HTML5 Web page and no output is displayed when you launch Listing 1.1 in a browser.

LISTING 1.1 Sample1.html

```
<!doctype html>
<html lang="en">
 <head>
  <meta charset="utf-8">
  <title>This is HTML5</title>
 </head>

 <body>
   <div id="outer"></div>
 <body>
</html>
```

Listing 1.1 contains an HTML5 <!DOCTYPE> element whose simple structure is very intuitive and easy to remember, especially in comparison to the syntax for an HTML4 <!DOCTYPE> element (try to construct one from memory!). This markup is backward-compatible: it triggers standards mode in all browsers that have standards mode (versus quirks mode) and it also tells the browser to use the special HTML5 parsing mode.

In addition, the <meta> tag and its attributes lang and charset attributes are simpler than their counterparts in earlier versions of HTML. Note that HTML5 supports the new syntax as well as the earlier syntax, so your existing HTML pages will be recognized in HTML5.

NEW HTML5 ELEMENTS

This section discusses some of the useful new elements in HTML5, which includes semantic-related elements, the <video> element, and the <audio> element. The new types for the <input> element are discussed in the section for HTML5 forms (later in this chapter). A modest knowledge of the new HTML5 tags is required in order to follow the examples in this book, so you can skim through this section if you do not require extensive knowledge of HTML5 elements.

Semantic Markup HTML5 Elements

HTML5 provides new elements for "semantic markup" that are designed to provide more meaningful structure in your HTML5 Web pages. Some of these new tags are: <section>, <article>, <aside>, <nav>, <header>, <canvas>, <video>, <audio>, <time>, <figure>, and <figcaption>.

For example, the HTML5 <section> tag can be used as a "container" for a document, whereas the HTML5 <article> tag is well-suited for representing the content of a newspaper article or a blog post. The HTML5 <header> tag and HTML5 <footer> tag represent the header and footer of an HTML5 <section> tag. The HTML5 <aside> tag contains information that is somewhat related to the primary content of a Web page (similar in nature to a "by the way" type of comment).

The HTML5 <nav> tag supports navigation for a section of a document in a Web page. Other new tags include the HTML5 <dialog> tag for marking up conversations and the HTML5 <figure> tag for associating a caption for videos or graphics (which is useful for search engines).

The semantics of these tags are straightforward, yet there are some subtler aspects that you will learn as you gain experience with HTML5 Web pages.

Semantic markup also includes WAI-ARIA (Web Accessibility Initiative-Accessible Rich Internet Applications). In brief, WAI-ARIA is a "bridging" technology that clarifies semantics of assistive technologies. The WAI-ARIA specification describes the roles, states, and properties that define accessible user interface elements, which are described (along with aria-* attributes on HTML elements) here:

http://dev.w3.org/html5/spec/wai-aria.html

Article Versus Section: How Are They Used?

The semantics of the HTML5 <article> element and the HTML5 <section> are complex, partly because they can be nested in each other: an <article> element can contain one or more <section> elements, and each of those section elements can contain one or more `<article>` elements. While it's possible to devise a "hack" to disambiguate the logical relationship of these elements in a given HTML5 Web page, no standard convention exists right now. Another factor is the manner in which the Document Outlining Algorithm (which creates outlines in HTML Web pages) treats these two HTML elements. You can find information about this algorithm here:

http://coding.smashingmagazine.com/2011/08/16/html5-and-the-document-outlining-algorithm/.

For simple HTML5 Web pages, the `<article>` element and the `<section>` element will behave in a reasonable manner, but for more complex HTML5 Web pages, the results might be unexpected (or unwanted). Before you use the `<section>` and `<article>` elements for content in an HTML5 Web page, think of the logical relationship of the content in order to determine the structural layout of your HTML5 Web page. If there is any possibility for confusion, it might also be helpful to include a comment section to make it easier for other people to understand the rationale for the layout of your HTML5 Web page. In any case, it's worth spending some time learning about these elements and also about the Document Outlining Algorithm.

Why Use Semantic Markup?

There are at least two reasons for using semantic tags in your Web pages. First, semantic tags can help you understand the structure of a Web page and the purpose of a section of mark-up. Second, the use of semantic tags makes it easier for you to programmatically locate and manage sets of logically similar sections of code (such as `<nav>` elements, `<aside>` elements, and so forth). Third, screen-readers and search engines can use these tags to separate the content from navigation in a Web page. These are several of the more important reasons for using semantic markup, and you can probably think of other reasons as well.

Incidentally, jQuery Mobile uses custom attributes (which always start with the string "`data-`") as a way to embed data that can be accessed programmatically, and to a lesser extent, sort of "document" different sections of a Web page. Later in this section, you will see an example of a jQuery Mobile Web page that uses custom attributes.

A Simple Web Page with Semantic Markup

Listing 1.2 displays the contents of `SemanticMarkup1.html` that illustrates how to use HTML5 semantic markup.

LISTING 1.2 SemanticMarkup1.html

```
<!DOCTYPE HTML>
<html>
<head>
   <meta charset="utf-8">
   <title>Examples of HTML5 Semantic Markup </title>
 </head>
```

```
<body>
  <article> <!-- start article #1 -->
    <header>
      <h1>An HTML5 CSS3 Canvas Graphics Primer</h1>
    </header>

    <header>
        <aside style="font-size:larger;font-style:italic;color:red;
float:right;width:150px;">
          The book is available on Amazon as well as MercLearning.
        </aside>
<p>This book covers the features of HTML5 Canvas graphics and CSS3
graphics, and shows how to extend the power of CSS3 with SVG.<p>
<p>The material is accessible to people with basic knowledge of
HTML and JavaScript, and more advanced users will benefit from the
examples of sophisticated CSS3 2D/3D animation effects.</p>
<p>Learn how to create HTML5 web pages that use Canvas, CSS3, and
SVG to render 2D shapes and Bezier curves, create linear and radial
gradients, apply transforms to 2D shapes and JPG files, create
animation effects, and generate 2D/3D bar charts and line graphs.<p>

        <nav>
         <ul>
            <li><a href="http://www.amazon.ca/HTML5-Canvas-CSS3-
Graphics-Primer/dp/1936420341">Amazon Link</a></li>
            <li><a href="http://www.merclearning.com/titles/html5_
canvas_css3_graphics.html
">MercLearning Link</a></li>
          </ul>
        </nav>

        <details>
          <summary>More Details About the Book</summary>
<p>The code samples in this book run on WebKit-based browsers on
desktops and tablets. A companion DVD contains all the source code
and color graphics in the book.</p>
        </details>
      </header>

    <section>
      <h3>Other Books by the Author</h3>
      <article> <!-- start article #2 -->
        <p>Previous books include: Java Graphics Programming, Web
2.0 Fundamentals, SVG Fundamentals, and Pro Android Flash.<p>
        <footer>
          <p>Posted by: Oswald Campesato</p>
        </footer>
       <details>
        <summary>More Details</summary>
        <p>Contact me for more detailed information</p>
       </details>
      </article> <!-- end article #2 -->

      <article> <!-- start article #3 -->
<p>SVCC (Silicon Valley Code Camp) is the biggest free code camp
in the world, and also a great way to meet like-minded people who
are interested in the latest trends in technology.</p>
```

```
    <img src="ThreeSpheres1.png" width="200" height="100" />
    </article> <!-- end article #3 -->
  </section>
  </article> <!-- end article #1 -->
 </body>
</html>
```

The <body> tag in Listing 1.2 contains an HTML5 <article> tag that in turn contains two HTML5 <header> tags, where the second HTML5 <header> tag contains an HTML5 <aside>. The next part of Listing 1.2 contains an HTML5 <nav> element with three HTML <a> links for navigation.

Figure 1.1 displays the result of rendering the Web page `Semantic-Markup1.html` in a Chrome Browser.

An HTML5 CSS3 Canvas Graphics Primer

This book covers the features of HTML5 Canvas graphics and CSS3 graphics, and shows how to extend the power of CSS3 with SVG. *The book is available on*

The material is accessible to people with basic knowledge of HTML and JavaScript, and more advanced users will benefit from the examples of sophisticated CSS3 2D/3D animation effects. *Amazon as well as MercLearning.*

Learn how to create HTML5 pages that use Canvas, CSS3, and SVG to render 2D shapes and Bezier curves, create linear and radial gradients, apply transforms to 2D shapes and JPG files, create animation effects, and generate 2D/3D bar charts and line graphs.

- Amazon Link
- MercLearning Link

▶ More Details About the Book

Other Books by the Author

Previous books include: Java Graphics Programming, Web 2.0 Fundamentals, SVG Fundamentals, and Pro Android Flash.

Posted by: Oswald Campesato

▶ More Details

SVCC (Silicon Valley Code Camp) is the biggest free code camp in the world, and also a great way to meet like-minded people who are interested in the latest trends in technology.

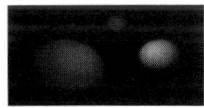

FIGURE 1.1 An HTML5 Web Page with Semantic Markup in a Chrome Browser.

Custom Data Attributes in HTML5

HTML5 supports custom data attributes, which effectively enables you to write HTML5 Web pages in which you can store custom data that is private to the Web page or application.

Listing 1.3 displays the contents of the Web page `CustomAtributes1.html` that illustrates some of the custom attributes that are available in jQuery Mobile.

Note: Listing 1.3 only displays how you would structure an HTML5 Web page that uses jQuery, and the code to render an actual header and footer in a jQuery Mobile Web page is discussed in Chapter 8.

LISTING 1.3 CustomAttributes1.html

```
<!doctype html>
<html lang="en">
  <head>
   <meta charset="utf-8">
       <title>Hello World from jQueryMobile</title>
  </head>

  <body>
    <div id="page1" data-role="page">
      <header data-role="header" data-position="fixed">
        <h1>jQuery Mobile</h1>
      </header>

      <div class="content" data-role="content">
        <h3>Content Area</h3>
      </div>

      <footer data-role="footer" data-position="fixed">
        <h3>Fixed Footer</h3>
      </footer>
    </div>
  </body>
</html>
```

Listing 1.3 displays the structure of an HTML5 Web page for jQuery Mobile, but it is incomplete because it does not contain references to any jQuery JavaScript files or CSS stylesheets. The purpose of Listing 1.3 is to shows you the layout of a simple jQuery Mobile page, which in this case consists of one so-called "page view," along with some of the custom data attributes that are common in jQuery Mobile. We will delve into jQuery Mobile Web pages in greater detail in Chapters 8 and 9.

THE HTML5 TEMPLATE ELEMENT

If you have worked with server-side templating or client-side templating, the HTML5 <template> element will be very familiar to you. If you are new to templating techniques, the basic idea is that the HTML5 <template> element enables you to define a template with variables whose values are populated at "run-time." You can programmatically test whether or not a browser supports the <template> element and then use conditional logic to manipulate a custom HTML5 <template> element with the following code block:

```
function supportsTemplate() {
  return 'content' in document.createElement('template');
}

if(supportsTemplate()) {
  // use the custom HTML5 template here
} else {
  // use old templating techniques
}
```

```
<template id="myTemplate">
  <img src="" alt="my sample image">
  <div class="comment"></div>
</template>
```

Next, activate the preceding template (whose `id` attribute has the value `myTemplate`) by creating a deep copy of its `.content` using `cloneNode()` method. Note that `.content` is a read-only property, and it references a `DocumentFragment` that contains a template. The code block looks like this:

```
var tmpl = document.querySelector('#myTemplate');

// Populate the src attribute at run time
tmpl.content.querySelector('img').src = 'sample.png';

// clone and append to the <body> element
document.body.appendChild(tmpl.content.cloneNode(true));
```

The preceding code block clones the template, sets a value for the `src` attribute, and appends the populated template to the `<body>` element. Now that you have a basic understanding of the HTML5 template element, the next section discusses HTML5 Web Components, which are new to HTML5.

HTML5 WEB COMPONENTS

In simplified terms, HTML5 Web Components enables you to subclass existing HTML elements in order to define new components with custom functionality. A custom Web Component is defined as a HTML5 `Template` (discussed in the previous section) where you can also define custom listeners. Web Components enable you to define widgets that can be reused reliably, even if the internal details of the widget are altered.

The term "Web Components" usually involves these four concepts:

• templates with "blocks" of markup
• decorators that apply templates and use CSS to perform changes to Web pages
• custom elements that are defined by authors
• the "shadow DOM" that specifies how presentation and behavior of decorators and custom elements fit together in the DOM tree

The following example illustrates how to create a custom HTML5 Web Component.

You can find examples of custom Web Components here:

https://dvcs.w3.org/hg/webcomponents/raw-file/tip/samples/index.html

As you can see, HTML5 `Web Components` is a promising technology, and it will be interesting to see the new toolkits with support for this functionality, along with the Web applications that leverage those toolkits. In addition, some of the existing toolkits will undoubtedly available themselves of HTML5

`Web Components`, which in turn will enable existing applications to leverage this new functionality in HTML5.

Additional details about Web Components are discussed in these two Websites:

http://www.w3.org/TR/components-intro/
http://www.chromium.org/blink/web-components

HTML5 WEB COMPONENTS LIBRARIES

Polymer (formerly called Toolkitchen) is an open source project that is based on HTML5 `Web Components`, and its homepage is here:

http://www.polymer-project.org/

This project is in an early stage, and you can read the FAQ here:

http://www.polymer-project.org/faq.html

Another Web Component library is X-Tag, and its homepage is here:

http://www.x-tags.org/

According to the home page of the X-Tag library:
"X-Tag is a small JavaScript library, created and supported by Mozilla, that brings Web Components Custom Element capabilities to all modern browsers."
A third interesting collection of Web Components is here:

http://web.chemdoodle.com/demos

This concludes the discussion of HTML5 Web Components. The next portion of this chapter discusses HTML5 global attributes and HTML5 event attributes, both of which are new to HTML5.

ADDITIONAL NEW FUNCTIONALITY IN HTML5

HTML5 provides new global attributes that you can apply to many HTML elements, some of which are:

- contenteditable
- contextmenu
- draggable
- dropzone
- hidden
- spellcheck

The preceding global attributes can be used on any HTML element.
HTML5 also provides new event attributes, which indicate an event that might happen when the page is loaded. The new HTML5 event attributes include:

- onabort fires when an action is aborted
- onbeforeonload, onbeforeonunload, and onunload fire before an element loads or unloads and as an element unloads

- oncontextmenu fires when the context menu is triggered
- ondrag, ondragend, ondragenter, ondragleave, ondragstart, and ondrop fire when various drag-and-drop actions occur
- onerror and onmessage fire when errors or messages are triggered
- onscroll fires when users scroll the browser scroll bar
- onresize fires when an element is resized

Perform an Internet search to find code snippets that illustrate how to use the new global attributes and new event attributes in HTML5 Web pages.

HTML5 VALIDATORS

HTML5 validators enable you to test HTML5 Web pages and mobile applications. Many types of validators for Web applications are available, including:

- HTML validators (test the validity of your HTML)
- Accessibility validators (test Web pages to determine how well they can be read by screen readers)
- Code validators (check your scripts, CSS, and API calls for accuracy)
- Mobile validators (provide advice for improving pages for mobile devices, and often act as emulators)

In addition to the preceding list, there are other tools that can evaluate the "friendliness" of your Website, such as:

- the W3C mobileOK Checker (*http://validator.w3.org/mobile*)
- mobiReady (*http://ready.mobi*)

Both the W3C mobileOK Checker and mobiReady analyze live Web pages on the Internet, and then provide a report that describes how they would perform on mobile devices.

HTML5 WAI ARIA

WAI-ARIA (Web Accessibility Initiative-Accessible Rich Internet Applications) is a W3C specification that specifies how to increase the accessibility of Web pages (including dynamic content) and user interface components developed with Ajax, HTML, JavaScript, and related technologies.

Although WAI-ARIA predates HTML5, the HTML5 WAI-ARIA specification defines support for accessible Web applications, which involves markup extensions that are often attributes of HTML5 elements. Web developers can use these markup extensions to obtain more information about screen readers and other assistive technologies.

As a simple example, consider the following code snippet of an enhanced HTML `<li>` element from the ARIA specification illustrates the use of the `role` and `aria-checked` attributes:

```
<li role="menuitemcheckbox" aria-checked="true">
  <img src="checked.gif" role="presentation" alt="">
  <!-- note: additional scripts required to toggle image source -->
  Sort by Last Modified
</li>
```

The two new attributes in the preceding code snippet have no impact on the manner in which browsers render the `<li>` element. Browsers that support ARIA will add OS-specific accessibility information to the rendered `<li>` element, and enable screen readers to read information aloud in a contextual manner.

If you are planning to use jQuery and also to support ARIA, there is a jQuery plugin that provides ARIA support here:

http://webcloud.se/code/jQuery-Collapse/

You can get more information about the WAI-AIA specification here:

http://www.w3.org/TR/wai-aria/
http://www.techrepublic.com/blog/webmaster/a-checklist-for-web-accessibility-issues/2626

HTML5 APIS IN EXPERIMENTAL STATUS

This section covers HTML5 APIs in the early stage of the W3C process, so they are covered lightly.

The *CSS Compositing* specification is an "Editor's Note" and work in progress, and it has recently appeared in the WebKit "nightlies," which means that as this book goes to print, the code will probably be part of the mainline for WebKit. Compositing pertains to combining shapes of different elements into a single image. Previous versions of SVG used Simple Alpha Compositing, and the latest specification defines a new compositing model that expands upon the Simple Alpha Compositing model. Full details are here:

http://dvcs.w3.org/hg/FXTF/raw-file/tip/compositing/index.html

Mozilla *Firefox OS* (previously called B2G (Boot to Gecko)) is intended to be a new open mobile ecosystem based on HTML5. Mobile devices that run Firefox OS will support HTML5 Web pages that can access all the capabilities of mobile devices. The operating system (which uses Firefox) will enable developers to access the capabilities of these mobile devices as part of HTML5 applications. More details are here:

https://blog.mozilla.org/blog/2012/07/02/firefox-mobile-os/

The *Voice Recognition* (TTS) specification involves converting text to speech, which involves CSS properties for declaratively controlling the rendering of documents via speech synthesis, along with optional audio cues. Full details are here:

http://www.w3.org/TR/css3-speech

OTHER UPCOMING HTML5 FEATURES

There are several sets of APIs that are under development and discussion at the W3C, some of which are listed here:

- the Shadow DOM
- the Pointer Lock API (game-oriented)
- the Gamepad API (game-oriented)

Since these APIs are developmental in nature, this section only provides links for obtaining information about these APIs.

The Shadow DOM specification is here:

http://www.w3.org/TR/shadow-dom

The specification for the Pointer Lock API (WebApps Working Group) is here:

http://dvcs.w3.org/hg/pointerlock/raw-file/tip/index.html

You can get information about the GamePad API here:

https://dvcs.w3.org/hg/gamepad/raw-file/default/gamepad.html

Some experimental GamePad code (Firefox only) is here:

https://developer.mozilla.org/en/API/Gamepad/Using_Gamepad_API

The newest version of the DOM is DOM4, and the specification details are here:

http://www.w3.org/TR/domcore/

In addition, the specification for DOM4 events is here:

http://html5labs.interoperabilitybridges.com/dom4events/

WEBP IMAGE FORMAT

Google developed the WebP image format, whose smaller size for images makes it more efficient in terms of rendering Web pages. In particular, Facebook has experimented with the WebP format, which could lead to significant cost savings. However, Windows, OS X, Photoshop, and other software do not recognize the WebP image format. Consequently, Facebook users (among others) will not be able to edit images in a WebP image format.

http://news.cnet.com/8301-1023_3-57580664-93/facebook-tries-googles-webp-image-format-users-squawk/

MOBILE SUPPORT FOR HTML5

A very good Website that lists the HTML5 features (including the ones that have been discussed in this chapter) that are supported by mobile browsers is here:

http://mobilehtml5.org/

Currently, Safari on iOS supports 28 features whereas the Android supports 24 features (other browsers are listed as well).

Another good Website that provides test results of HTML-related features on various mobile devices is here:

http://www.quirksmode.org/mobile/

The preceding Website is maintained by Peter Paul Koch (who is often called PPK), and he maintains Web pages with many test results, along with blog posts expressing his views about trends in HTML5 and the mobile space.

ADDITIONAL CODE SAMPLES ON THE DVD

The HTML5 Web page `DragDrop1.html` (which uses `DragDrop.css` and `DragDrop.js`) shows you how to handle drag-and-drop functionality in "pure" JavaScript. Chapter 8 contains the jQuery version of the code for drag-and-drop functionality.

SUMMARY

This chapter provided an overview of several HTML5-related techniques for managing and persisting user-provided data using HTML5 `Forms`. In this chapter, you learned how to do the following:

- create HTML5 Web pages
- use new semantic markup
- distinguish between `<section>` and `<article>` tags
- use custom data attributes
- use online tools for HTML5 development

STORAGE, DATABASES, GEOLOCATION, AND OFFLINE APPS

This chapter introduces you to several HTML5 technologies, including HTML5 Web storage, Web databases, Geolocation, and Offline Applications. Web Storage supports `LocalStorage` for persistent storage and `SessionStorage` for temporary storage of session-related information. Web databases include WebSQL (which is not covered here because development stopped in November, 2010) and IndexedDB. Geolocation enables users to share their current location, and as you will see later in this chapter, their location may be determined by several methods. Finally, Offline Web Applications enable users to work on an application even when they are disconnected from the Internet. When users do have access to the Internet, their data changes are synchronized so that everything is in a consistent state.

You can launch all the code samples in this chapter in a WebKit browser on a laptop, which is more convenient that launching them as mobile applications. However, you can use the techniques in Chapter 2 to easily create the corresponding hybrid HTML5 Android mobile applications by using PhoneGap in Eclipse or by manually modifying a basic Android application that is created in Eclipse.

USING HTML5 WEB STORAGE

The essence of HTML5 Web Storage is that it provides a very simple way to store as key/value pairs, along with a set of APIs for managing your data. In addition to storing simple key/value pairs, you can create a value string consisting of a JSON expression that contains a set of name/value pairs. You can serialize the JSON data before storing it in Web Storage, and then deserialize that JSON data whenever you retrieve it from Web Storage.

Although there is no query language for local storage, you can determine the number of keys in local storage through `localstorage.length`, which you can use as the maximum value for a loop that iterates through the items in local storage. As a simple example, the following code block iterates through the keys in local storage and checks for the values that start with the string `Emp`:

```
var itemCount = localStorage.length, i=0, key="", value="";

while ( ++i < itemCount ) {
      // retrieve the value of the current key
      key = localStorage.key( i );

      // retrieve the value associated with the current key
      value = localStorage.getItem( key );

      if(value.substr(0,3) == "Emp") {
         // do something with this element
      }
}
```

In addition to storing strings in Web Storage, you can also store JSON data, as shown here:

http://www.codeproject.com/Articles/361428/HTML5-Web-Storage

The advantage of HTML5 Web Storage (both local and session) is the simplicity of the APIs. However, there are some limitations of HTML5 Web Storage:

1) an initial platform-specific limit for data
2) no transactional support
3) no query language for accessing structured data

Browsers often have their own mechanism for increasing the amount of available storage after the initial limit is exceeded (the details of which vary among browsers).

HTML5 Web Storage Versus Cookies

An HTTP cookie is a set of key/value pairs that is used to communicate with a Web server. Cookies are included in an HTTP request header, provided that the cookie data is still valid and the requested domain and path also match the original cookie domain and path. Although cookies are convenient, they do have some drawbacks, such as their size and limits (typically 4K bytes and 300 cookies), performance, and security.

Local Storage and Session Storage are intended to provide support for storing a larger amount of data (megabytes instead of kilobytes), storing data beyond a current session, and also support for transactions that occur in multiple browser windows simultaneously, all of which makes HTML5 Web Storage a more powerful technology than cookies.

HTML5 Web Storage and Security

The APIs are subject to the "same origin" policy, where origins are determined by domain name (not the underlying IP address). In simplified terms, if you have a unique domain name, you have control over which pages see your data, even on shared hosting. By default, your locally stored data is not shared among subdomains. This security policy is also used to define security for the XMLHTTPRequest object. More information about the "same origin" policy is here:

https://developer.mozilla.org/en/Same_origin_policy_for_JavaScript

Now that you have a basic understanding of Local Storage, the next section contains a code sample that illustrates how to store text strings (consisting of concatenated words) in Local Storage.

AN EXAMPLE OF HTML5 LOCAL STORAGE

The example in this section uses local storage so that we can persist the data in the multi-lingual dictionary. If you decide to replace local storage with session storage, the data will be available only for the current browser session (hence the name "session storage").

Listing 2.1 displays the contents of `MultiLingualForm2.html` that illustrates how to create and manage our data in local storage.

LISTING 2.1 MultiLingualForm2.html

```
<html lang="en">
<head>
<meta charset="utf-8">
 <title>Our Multi-Lingual Dictionary</title>
 <link rel="stylesheet" media="screen" href="MultiLingualForm2.css" />

<script>
 function displayItem() {
    var dictionary  = document.forms["dictionary"];
    var english     = dictionary.english.value;
    var storageItem = localStorage.getItem(english);

    var splitItem   = item.split(":");
    var english     = splitItem[0];
    var japanese    = splitItem[1];
    var spanish     = splitItem[2];
    var french      = splitItem[3];
    var italian     = splitItem[4];

    dictionary.english.value  = english;
    dictionary.japanese.value = japanese;
    dictionary.spanish.value  = spanish;
```

```
      dictionary.french.value   = french;
      dictionary.italian.value  = italian;
   }

   function addWord() {
      var dictionary = document.forms["dictionary"];

      var english    = dictionary.english.value;
      var japanese   = dictionary.japanese.value;
      var spanish    = dictionary.spanish.value;
      var french     = dictionary.french.value;
      var italian    = dictionary.italian.value;
      var incomplete = 0;

      var concatenated =  english + ":" + japanese + ":" +
                          spanish + ":" + french + ":" +
                          italian;

      if(english == ""||japanese == ""||spanish == ""||
         french == ""||italian == "")
      {
         ++incomplete;
   console.log("Skipping incomplete/empty row!");
         return;
      }

      try {
         localStorage.setItem(english, concatenated);
         alert("added new word: "+ concatenated);
         clearFields();

         // append new words to dropdown list
         option = new Option( english );
         wordList.options[wordList.length] = option;
      } catch (e) {
         if (e == QUOTA_EXCEEDED_ERR) {
            alert("Local Storage Quota exceeded");
            // you can clear local storage here:
            //clearLocalStorage();
         }
      }
   }

   function clearFields() {
      var dictionary = document.forms["dictionary"];

      dictionary.english.value  = "";
      dictionary.japanese.value = "";
      dictionary.spanish.value  = "";
      dictionary.french.value   = "";
      dictionary.italian.value  = "";
   }

   function clearLocalStorage() {
      localStorage.clear();
      populateDropDownList();
```

```
    }

    // remove the options from the list
    function removeItemsFromDropDownList() {
      while ( wordList.options.length ) wordList.options[0] = null;
    }

    function createTestData() {
      removeItemsFromDropDownList();
      clearLocalStorage();

      localStorage.setItem("eat", "eat:taberu:comer:manger:mangiare");
      localStorage.setItem("go",  "go:iku:andar:aller:andare");
      localStorage.setItem("buy", "buy:kau:comprar:acheter:comprare");
    }

    function populateDropDownList() {
      // the length property contains the item count in the storage
      var i = -1, key, itemCount, items = {};

      createTestData();
      itemCount = localStorage.length;

// option = new Option( "eat:taberu:comer:manger:mangiare" );
// wordList.options[wordList.length] = option;

      while ( ++i < itemCount ) {
         // retrieve the value of the current key
         key = localStorage.key( i );

         // retrieve the value of the current item
         items[key] = localStorage.getItem( key );

         option = new Option( key );

         // Append to existing options
         wordList.options[wordList.length] = option;
      }

      // Ensure option 0 is selected
      wordList.selectedIndex = 0;
   }
</script>
</head>

<body onLoad="populateDropDownList()">
  <h1>Our Multi-Lingual Dictionary</h1>
  <form id="dictionary" onsubmit="return false;">
  <form>
   <fieldset>
    <div>
      <button id="add" onClick="addWord()">Add New Words</button>
    </div>

    <div>
      <label for="english">English:</label>
```

```
    <input type="text" name="english" id="english" />
  </div>

  <div>
    <label for="japanese">Japanese:</label>
    <input type="text" name="japanese" id="japanese" />
  </div>

  <div>
    <label for="spanish">Spanish:</label>
    <input type="text" name="spanish" id="spanish" />
  </div>

  <div>
    <label for="french">French:</label>
    <input type="text" name="french" id="french" />
  </div>

  <div>
    <label for="italian">Italian:</label>
    <input type="text" name="italian" id="italian" />
  </div>

  <div>
    <button id="clear1" onClick="clearFields()">Clear Input
Fields</button>
    <button id="clear2" onClick="clearLocalStorage()">Clear
Local Storage</button>
  </div>

  <label for="none">The List of Words in Our Dictionary:</label>
  <br />
  <div>
  <select id="wordList" onchange="update()">
    <option value=""></option>
  </select>
  </div>
  </fieldset>
  </form>
</body>
</html>
```

Listing 2.1 contains the JavaScript functions for handling associated functionality. Whenever a new row is added, the JavaScript function addWord() performs a concatenation of the words in that row, with a semi-colon (":") as the delimiter between words, as shown here:

```
var concatenated =  english + ":" + japanese + ":" +
                    spanish + ":" + french + ":" +
                    italian;
```

Next, the concatenated string concatenated is stored as part of a "dictionary" in local storage in a try/catch block with the following line of code:

```
localStorage.setItem(english, concatenated);
```

Keep in mind that the preceding code snippet is equivalent to this snippet:

```
localStorage["eat"] = "eat:taberu:comer:manger:mangiare";
```

Conversely, when the words are retrieved from the dictionary, the JavaScript function `displayItem()` will "split" each concatenated string into the words that are stored in the concatenated string, and then the individual words are displayed in the corresponding language field.

The JavaScript function `displayItem()` displays a word in each input field for each of the specified languages. The JavaScript functions `clearFields()` and `clearLocalStorage()` remove the data from the input fields and from the dictionary in local storage.

Note that each time the HTML page is loaded, the `populateDropDownList()` function is invoked, which creates some test data (via the JavaScript function `createTestData()`) and then populates the dropdown list with the words that are in the dictionary in local storage, as shown here:

```
localStorage.setItem("eat",  "eat:taberu:comer:manger:mangiare");
localStorage.setItem("go",   "go:iku:andar:aller:andare");
localStorage.setItem("buy",  "buy:kau:comprar:acheter:comprare");
```

Finally, the JavaScript function `removeItemsFromDropDownList()` removes the data from the dropdown list with this line of code:

```
while ( wordList.options.length ) wordList.options[0] = null;
```

LISTING 2.2 MultiLingualForm2.css

```css
fieldset {
    float: left;
    border: 2; width: 50%;
    background: #F88;}

div label {
    float: left;
    border: 0; width: 20%;
    background: #FF0;
    border-radius: 6px;
    box-shadow: 0 0 4px #222222;
}

label {
    float: left;
    border: 0; width: 60%;
    background: #0AD;
    border-radius: 6px;
    box-shadow: 0 0 4px #222222;
}

input {
    border: 0; width: 40%;
    border: 2px solid white;
```

```
    background: #F44;
    border-radius: 6px;
    box-shadow: 0 0 4px #333333;
}

button, select {
    font-size: 16px;
    border: 1px solid white;
    background: #CCC;
    border-radius: 6px;
    box-shadow: 0 0 4px #222222;
    width: 60%;
    padding: 6px;
}
```

Listing 2.2 displays CSS3 selectors for four HTML elements: `fieldset`, `label`, `input`, and the `submit` button. The selectors specify attributes such as the border, width, padding, and rounded corners for the corresponding HTML elements. For example, the CSS3 selector for the HTML `[[label]]` element specifies yellow (#FF0) for the `background` and a `border-radius` of 6 pixels, as shown here:

```
background: #FF0;
border-radius: 6px;
```

Similar comments apply to the other CSS selectors in Listing 2.2, whose content is similar to the CSS selector for the `[[label]]` element.

Figure 2.1 displays the rendered HTML5 Web page `MultiLingualForm2.html`, which creates a vivid effect because of the CSS3 selectors in the CSS stylesheet.

The example in the next section also uses an HTML5 Form that handles data input, but this time the data will be stored in an HTML5 database instead of online local storage.

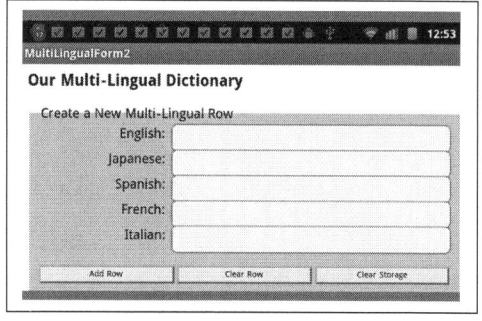

FIGURE 2.1 An HTML5 Form with CSS3 on a Sprint Nexus S 4G with Android ICS.

Incidentally, in addition to storing simple text strings in HTML5 local storage, you can also store images and files, and you can get some useful information and code samples here:

https://hacks.mozilla.org/2012/02/saving-images-and-files-in-localstorage/

You can get the complete code for the preceding article from Github:

https://github.com/robnyman/robnyman.github.com/tree/master/html5demos/localstorage

Note that it's better to store images in `IndexedDB` because of size limitations for local storage.

HTML5 WEB DATABASES

In addition to using Web Storage for storing data, there are two databases that provide more robust functionality. The database that is actively being developed is `IndexedDB`, which has not been fully implemented in all modern browsers as this book goes to print.

Another database is `WebSQL`, but development on this database was discontinued in November, 2010. However, if you have a Web application that uses `WebSQL`, the following article provides useful information to help you migrate to `IndexedDB`:

http://www.html5rocks.com/en/tutorials/webdatabase/websql-indexeddb/

There are various open source projects available that provide database features for Web applications. For example, `html5sql` is a JavaScript module that focuses on sequential processing of SQL statements in a transaction, and its homepage is here:

http://html5sql.com/

With `html5sql` you can process SQL as a single statement string, as an array of strings or objects, or from a separate file that contains SQL statements.

Another open source project is the JavaScript database `TaffyDB`, and its homepage is here:

http://taffydb.com/

This open source project includes features such as update and insert, along with cross-browser support, and the ability to extend the database with your own functions. In addition, `TaffyDB` is compatible with multiple tookits, such as jQuery, YUI, and Dojo.

The next section introduces you to `IndexedDB` and shows you how to store text strings in an `IndexedDB` database.

HTML5 WEB STORAGE VERSUS `INDEXEDDB`

The first advantage of `IndexedDB` over HTML5 Web Storage is its capacity: `IndexedDB` has a larger limit (50MB quota in Firefox 4+), and when that limit is exceeded, Firefox prompts the user for permission to increase the maximum size. The manner in which the quota is increased depends on the browser (for desktops and mobile devices), so you need to look into the details for each browser if you are writing a cross-browser application.

Earlier in this chapter you saw an example of using `IndexedDB`, and its advantages and disadvantages are the opposite of the first two advantages of HTML5 Web Storage that are listed in a previous section. The choice between Web Storage and `IndexedDB` depends on the complexity of your data, the requirements for your application, and whether it's available on your list of target browsers.

WEB DATABASE AND MOBILE DEVICES

You can try to use the same techniques for mobile applications that you use for Web applications, but you will encounter similar constraints in both environments. Although you can use native code to access a database, the solution will be specific to each type of device. The choice that you make depends on the requirements of your application.

One cross-platform solution is to use CouchDB Mobile, which is the mobile version of CouchDB. Another mobile-based alternative is TouchDB, which is a lightweight database engine that is compatible with Apache CouchDB. The creator of TouchDB makes the analogy that "if CouchDB is MySQL, then TouchDB is SQLite." An Android port and an iOS port of TouchDB are available here:

https://github.com/couchbaselabs/TouchDB-Android
https://github.com/couchbaselabs/TouchDB-iOS

GEOLOCATION

Geolocation allows users to share their current location, and their location may be determined by the following methods:

- Cell tower
- GPS hardware on the device
- IP address
- Wireless network connection

The actual method that is used depends on the browser and the capabilities of the device. The browser then determines the location and passes it back to the Geolocation API. Note that the W3C Geolocation specification mentions that there is no guarantee that the Geolocation API returns the device's actual location.

The `geolocation` object is a child object of `window.navigator`, and you can check if your browser supports `geolocation` with the following type of code block:

```
if(window.navigator.geolocation) {
  // geolocation supported
} else {
  // geolocation not supported
}
```

The W3C Geolocation API enables you to obtain Geolocation information in a browser session that is running on a device. The Geolocation object is available in the global `window.navigator` object, accessed via `window.navigator.geolocation`.

Note that the Geolocation API requires users to allow a Web application to access location information.

The Geolocation object contains the following three methods:

- `getCurrentPosition(successCallback, errorCallback, options)`
- `watchPosition(successCallback, errorCallback, options)`
- `clearWatch(watchId)`

The method `getCurrentPosition()` tries to get Geolocation information, and then calls the first method if it's successful, otherwise it calls the second method in its argument list.

The method `watchPosition()` obtains the Geolocation at regular intervals; success and failure are handled through the two JavaScript methods in its list of arguments.

Finally, the method `clearWatch(watchId)` stops the watch process based on the value of `watchId`.

The major difference between the two methods is that the `watchPosition()` method will return a value immediately upon being called which uniquely identifies that watch operation.

A table that displays support for Geolocation on desktop and mobile browsers is here:

http://caniuse.com/geolocation

Obtain a User's Position with `getCurrentPosition()`

The `PositionOptions` object is an optional parameter that can be passed to the `getCurrentPosition()` method, which is also an optional parameter to the `watchPosition()` method. All of the properties in the `PositionOptions` object are optional as well.

For example, you can define an instance of a `PositionOptions` object by means of the following JavaScript code block:

```
var options = {
  enableHighAccuracy: true,
  maximumAge: 60000,
  timeout: 45000
};
```

Next, we can invoke the getCurrentPosition() method by specifying a JavaScript success function, a JavaScript error function, and the previously defined options variable, as shown here:

```
navigator.geolocation.getCurrentPosition(successCallback,
                                         errorCallback,
                                         options);
```

Track a User's Position with watchPosition()

This method is useful when an application requires an updated position each time that a device changes location. The watch operation is an asynchronous operation that is invoked as shown here:

```
var watcher = null;
var options = { enableHighAccuracy: true, timeout: 30000 };

if (window.navigator.geolocation) {
   watcher = navigator.geolocation.watchPosition(
               successCallback,errorCallback, options);
} else {
   alert('Your browser does not support geolocation.');
}

function successCallback(position) {
   console.log("Success obtaining the device location");
}

// Error obtaining the location
function errorCallback(error) {
   console.log("Error obtaining the device location");
}
```

If your browser supports Geolocation, the JavaScript variable watcher is initialized via an invocation of the watchPosition() method of the geolocation object. Notice that the JavaScript functions successCallback() and errorCallback() for handling success or failure, respectively (in our case these functions simply display a message in you browser's console).

The W3C Geolocation API provides a method for clearing a watch operation by passing a watchId to the clearWatch() method, as shown here:

```
navigator.geolocation.clearWatch(watcher);
```

After creating a new watch operation, you can remove that watch after successfully retrieving the position of a device, as shown here:

```
var watcher = null;
var options = {enableHighAccuracy: true,timeout: 45000 };

if (window.navigator.geolocation) {
watcher = navigator.geolocation.watchPosition(successCallback,
            errorCallback, options);
} else {
```

```
alert('Your browser does not support geolocation.');
}

function successCallback(position) {
   navigator.geolocation.clearWatch(watcher);
   // Do something with a location here
}
```

As you can see, the JavaScript `successCallback()` function does nothing more than "clearing" the Javascript variable `watcher`; the key point is that you will continue receiving information until you clear this variable.

Chapter 8 contains a code sample that shows you how to use Geolocation with jQuery Mobile. In addition, the DVD contains the HTML Web page `JQGeolocation1.html` with `geoPlugin` (which is not a jQuery plugin):

http://www.geoplugin.com

However, if you prefer to use a jQuery plugin for Geolocation, there are several available, including this one:

http://mobile.tutsplus.com/tutorials/mobile-web-apps/html5-geolocation/

HTML5 OFFLINE WEB APPLICATIONS

The purpose of Offline Web Applications is simple: users can work on an application even when they are disconnected from the Internet. When users do have access to the Internet, their data changes are synchronized so that everything is in a consistent state.

A Website that contains demos, additional links, and tutorial-like information is here:

http://appcachefacts.info/

The Manifest File

The HTML5 specification requires a so-called "manifest file" (with `app-cache` as the suggested suffix) and a MIME type of `text/cache-manifest` that contains the following three sections:

CACHE (the list of files that are going to be cached)
NETWORK (the files that can only be accessed online)
FALLBACK (specifies the resource to display when users try to access non-cached resources)

As a simple example, Listing 2.4 displays the contents of a sample manifest file called `MyApp.appcache`.

LISTING 2.4 *MyApp.appcache*

```
CACHE MANIFEST
# Verson 1.0.0
CACHE:
```

```
Index.html
Cachedstuff.html
Mystyle.css
Myimage.jpg

NETWORK:
*
FALLBACK:
/ noncached.html
```

You must ensure that the manifest file is served with the following MIME type:

```
text/cache-manifest
```

Second, every Web page that uses offline functionality must reference the manifest file at the top of the Web page:

```
<html lang="en" manifest="mymanifest.appcache">
```

If you have a Web page that is hosted by a provider, you can verify that the Web page contains the correct MIME type by issuing the following type of command:

```
curl -I http://www.myprovider.com/mymanifest.appcache
```

Detecting Online and Offline Status

The simplest way to determine whether or not an application is offline in an HTML5 Web page is with the following code snippet:

```
if(navigator.onLine) {
  // application is online
} else {
  // application is offline
}
```

For mobile applications that uses jQuery Mobile, you can use the following type of code block:

```
$(document).bind("offline", function() {

  // application is offline

}
```

Binding the offline event as shown in the preceding code block is useful for handling situations whereby an application goes offline while users are actively viewing an application. In addition, you would send data to a server only when you are online, and store data locally via HTML5 LocalStorage when you are offline.

Another technique for handling online and offline events that works in Firefox 3 (you can test for its support for other browsers) is shown here:

```
document.body.addEventListener("offline", function () {
   // do something here
}, false);

document.body.addEventListener("online", function () {
   // do something else here
}, false);
```

The jQuery plugin jquery-offline is a cross-browser plugin that enables you to use jQuery syntax for Offline Applications, and its homepage is here:

https://github.com/wycats/jquery-offline

SUMMARY

This chapter provided an overview of several HTML5-related techniques for managing and persisting user-provided data using HTML5 Forms. In this chapter, you learned how to perform the following:

- save data in a persistent manner to local storage
- save data in a persistent manner to an online database
- work with Geolocation
- work with Offline Applications

INTRODUCTION TO CSS3

This chapter introduces various aspects of CSS3, such as 2D/3D graphics and 2D/3D animation. In some cases, CSS3 concepts are presented without code samples due to space limitations; however, those concepts are included because it's important for you to be aware of their existence. By necessity, this chapter assumes that you have a moderate understanding of CSS, which means that you know how to set properties in CSS selectors. If you are unfamiliar with CSS selectors, there are many introductory articles available through an Internet search. If you are convinced that CSS operates under confusing and seemingly arcane rules, then it's probably worth your while to read an online article about CSS box rules, after which you will have a better understanding of the underlying logic of CSS.

The first part of this chapter discusses browser-specific prefixes for CSS3 selectors, as well as pseudo-classes and relational symbols that you can use in conjunction with attributes in a selector. The second part of this chapter contains code samples that illustrate how to create shadow effects, how to render rectangles with rounded corners, and also how to use linear gradients (a radial gradient sample is on the DVD). The third part of this chapter covers CSS3 transforms (scale, rotate, skew, and translate), along with code samples that illustrate how to apply transforms to HTML elements and to JPG files. The third part of this chapter covers CSS3 3D graphics and animation effects.

You can launch the code samples in this chapter in a WebKit-based browser on a desktop or a laptop; you can also view them on mobile devices, provided that you launch them in a browser that supports the CSS3 features that are used in the code samples. For your convenience, many of the code samples in this chapter are accompanied by screenshots of the code samples on an iPad3, a Sprint Nexus S 4G, and an Asus Prime Android ICS 10" tablet (both on Android ICS), which enables you to compare those screenshots with the corresponding images that are rendered on Webkit-based browsers on desktops and laptops.

CSS3 SUPPORT

Before we delve into the details of CSS3, there are two important details that you need to know about defining CSS3-based selectors for HTML pages. First, you need to know the CSS3 features that are available in different browsers. One of the best Websites for determining browser support for CSS3 features is here:

http://caniuse.com/

The preceding link contains tabular information regarding CSS3 support in IE, Firefox, Safari, Chrome, and Opera.

Another highly useful tool that checks for CSS3 feature support is `Enhance.js`, that tests browsers to determine whether or not they can support a set of essential CSS and JavaScript properties, and then delivering features to those browsers that satisfies the test. You can download `Enhance.js` here:

http://filamentgroup.com/lab/introducing_enhancejs_smarter_safer_apply_progressive_enhancement/

BROWSER-SPECIFIC PREFIXES FOR CSS3 PROPERTIES

The second detail that you need to know is that many CSS3 properties currently require browser-specific prefixes in order for them to work correctly. The prefixes `-ie-`, `-moz-`, and `-o-` are for Internet Explorer, Firefox, and Opera, respectively. As an illustration, the following code block shows examples of these prefixes:

```
-ie-webkit-border-radius: 8px;
-moz-webkit-border-radius: 8px;
-o-webkit-border-radius: 8px;
border-radius: 8px;
```

In your CSS selectors, specify the attributes with browser-specific prefixes before the "generic" attribute, which serves as a default choice in the event that the browser-specific attributes are not selected. The CSS3 code samples in this book contain `WebKit`-specific prefixes, which helps us keep the CSS stylesheets manageable in terms of size. If you need CSS stylesheets that work on multiple browsers (for current versions as well as older versions), there are essentially two options available. One option involves manually adding the CSS3 code with all the required browser-specific prefixes, which can be tedious to maintain and also error-prone. Another option is to use CSS toolkits or frameworks (discussed in the next chapter) that can programmatically generate the CSS3 code that contains all browser-specific prefixes.

One other point to keep in mind is that Blink (Google's fork of Chrome) will keep the (unprefixed) feature behind the "enable experimental Web platform features" flag in about:flags until the feature is ready to be enabled by default.

Finally, an extensive list of browser-prefixed CSS properties is here:

http://peter.sh/experiments/vendor-prefixed-css-property-overview/

QUICK OVERVIEW OF CSS3 FEATURES

CSS3 adopts a modularized approach for extending existing CSS2 functionality as well as supporting new functionality. As such, CSS3 can be logically divided into the following categories:

- Backgrounds/borders
- Color
- Media queries
- Multi-column layout
- Selectors

With CSS3, you can create boxes with rounded corners and shadow effects; create rich graphics effects using linear and radial gradients; detect portrait and landscape mode; detect the type of mobile device using media query selectors; and produce multi-column text rendering and formatting.

In addition, CSS3 enables you to define sophisticated node selection rules in selectors using pseudo-classes, first or last child (`first-child`, `last-child`, `first-of-type`, and `last-of-type`), and also pattern-matching tests for attributes of elements. Several sections in this chapter contain examples of how to create such selection rules.

CSS3 PSEUDO CLASSES, ATTRIBUTE SELECTION, AND RELATIONAL SYMBOLS

This brief section contains examples of some pseudo-classes, followed by snippets that show you how to select elements based on the relative position of text strings in various attributes of those elements. Although this section focuses on the `nth-child()` pseudo-class, you will become familiar with various other CSS3 pseudo-classes and in the event that you need to use those pseudo-classes, a link is provided at the end of this section which contains more information and examples that illustrate how to use them.

CSS3 supports an extensive and rich set of pseudo-classes, including `nth-child()`, along with some of its semantically related "variants," such as `nth-of-type()`, `nth-first-of-type()`, `nth-last-of-type()`, and `nth-last-child()`.

CSS3 also supports Boolean selectors (which are also pseudo-classes) such as `empty`, `enabled`, `disabled`, and `checked`, which are very useful for Form-related HTML elements. One other pseudo class is `not()`, which returns a set of elements that do not match the selection criteria.

CSS3 Pseudo Classes

The CSS3 `nth-child()` is a very powerful and useful pseudo-class, and it has the following form:

`nth-child`(put-your-keyword-or-linear-expression-here)

The following list provides various examples of using the `nth-child()` pseudo-class in order to match various subsets of child elements of an HTML `<div>` element (which can be substituted by other HTML elements as well):

`div:nth-child(1)`: matches the first child element
`div:nth-child(2)`: matches the second child element
`div:nth-child(even)`: matches the even child elements
`div:nth-child(odd)`: matches the odd child elements

The interesting and powerful aspect of the `nth-child()` pseudo-class is its support for linear expressions of the form $an+b$, where a is a positive integer and b is a non-negative integer, as shown here (using an HTML5 `<div>` element):

`div:nth-child(3n)`: matches every third child, starting from position 0
`div:nth-child(3n+1)`: matches every third child, starting from position 1
`div:nth-child(3n+2)`: matches every third child, starting from position 2

CSS3 Attribute Selection

You can specify CSS3 selectors that select HTML elements as well as HTML elements based on the value of an attribute of an HTML element using various regular expressions. CSS3 uses the meta-characters ^, $, and * (followed by the = symbol) in order to match an initial, terminal, or arbitrary position for a text string. If you are familiar with the Unix utilities `grep` and `sed`, as well as the `vi` text editor, then these meta-characters are very familiar to you. For example, the following selector selects `img` elements whose `src` attribute starts with the text string `sample1`, and then sets the `width` attribute and the `height` attribute of the selected img elements to `100px`:

```
img[src^="sample1"] {
  width: 100px; height: 100px;
}
```

The preceding CSS3 selector is useful when you want to set different dimensions to images based on the name of the images (`Sample`, `Shelly`, `Steve`, and so forth).

The following HTML `<img>` elements do not match the preceding selector:

```
<img src="3sample1" width="200" height="200" />
<img src="3ssample1" width="200" height="200" />
```

The following selector selects HTML img elements whose `src` attribute ends with the text string `png`, and then sets the `width` attribute and the `height` attribute of the selected img elements to `150px`:

```
img[src$="png"] {
  width: 150px; height: 150px;
}
```

The preceding CSS3 selector is useful when you want to set different dimensions to images based on the type of the images (`jpg`, `png`, `jpeg`, and so forth).

The following selector selects HTML img elements whose `src` attribute contains any occurrence of the text string `baby`, and then sets the `width` attribute and the `height` attribute of the selected HTML img elements to `200px`:

```
img[src*="baby"] {
  width: 200px; height: 200px;
}
```

The preceding CSS3 selector is useful when you want to set different dimensions to images based on the "classification" of the images (`mybaby`, `yourbaby`, `babygirl`, `babyboy`, and so forth).

If you want to learn more about patterns (and their descriptions) that you can use in CSS3 selectors, an extensive list is available here:

http://www.w3.org/TR/css3-selectors

This concludes part one of this chapter, and the next section delves into CSS3 graphics-oriented effects, such as rounded corners and shadow effects.

CSS3 SHADOW EFFECTS AND ROUNDED CORNERS

CSS3 shadow effects are useful for creating vivid visual effects with simple selectors. You can use shadow effects for text as well as rectangular regions. CSS3 also enables you to easily render rectangles with rounded corners, so you do not need JPG files in order to create this effect.

Specifying Colors with RGB and HSL

Before we delve into the interesting features of CSS3, you need to know how to represent colors. One method is to use (R, G, B) triples, which represent the Red, Green, and Blue components of a color. For instance, the triples (255, 0, 0), (255, 255, 0), and (0, 0, 255) represent the colors

Red, Yellow, and Blue. Other ways of specifying the color include: the hexadecimal triples (FF, 0, 0) and (FF, 0, 0); the decimal triple (100%,0,0); or the string #F00. You can also use (R,G,B,A), where the fourth component specifies the opacity, which is a decimal number between 0 (invisible) to 1 (opaque) inclusive.

However, there is also the HSL (Hue, Saturation, and Luminosity) representation of colors, where the first component is an angle between 0 and 360 (0 degrees is north), and the other two components are percentages between 0 and 100. For instance, (0, 100%, 50%), (120, 100%, 50%), and (240, 100%, 50%) represent the colors Red, Green, and Blue, respectively.

The code samples in this book use (R,G,B) and (R,G,B,A) for representing colors, but you can perform an Internet search to obtain more information regarding HSL.

CSS3 and Text Shadow Effects

A shadow effect for text can make a Web page look more vivid and appealing, and many Websites look better with shadow effects that are not overpowering for users (unless you specifically need to do so). Another point to keep in mind is to verify that the shadow effects in your code do not adversely affect the legibility of text.

Listing 3.1 displays the contents of the HTML5 page TextShadow1.html that illustrate how to render text with a shadow effect, and Listing 3.2 displays the contents of the CSS stylesheet TextShadow1.css that is referenced in Listing 3.1.

LISTING 3.1 TextShadow1.html

```
<!DOCTYPE html>
<html lang="en">
<head>
  <title>CSS Text Shadow Example</title>
  <meta charset="utf-8" />
  <link href="TextShadow1.css" rel="stylesheet" type="text/css">
</head>

<body>
  <div id="text1">Line One Shadow Effect</div>
  <div id="text2">Line Two Shadow Effect</div>
  <div id="text3">Line Three Vivid Effect</div>

  <div id="text4">
    <span class="dd">13</span>
    <span class="mm">August</span>
    <span class="yy">2011</span>
  </div>

  <div id="text5">
    <span class="dd">13</span>
    <span class="mm">August</span>
    <span class="yy">2011</span>
  </div>
```

```
 <div id="text6">
   <span class="dd">13</span>
   <span class="mm">August</span>
   <span class="yy">2011</span>
 </div>
</body>
</html>
```

The code in Listing 3.1 is straightforward: there is a reference to the CSS stylesheet `TextShadow1.css` that contains two CSS selectors. One selector specifies how to render the HTML `<div>` element whose `id` attribute has value `text1`, and the other selector matches the HTML `<div>` element whose `id` attribute is `text2`. Although the CSS3 `rotate()` function is included in this example, we'll defer a more detailed discussion of this function until later in this chapter.

LISTING 3.2 TextShadow1.css

```
#text1 {
  font-size: 24pt;
  text-shadow: 2px 4px 5px #00f;
}

#text2 {
  font-size: 32pt;
  text-shadow: 0px 1px 6px #000,
               4px 5px 6px #f00;
}

#text3 {
  font-size: 40pt;
  text-shadow: 0px 1px 6px  #fff,
               2px 4px 4px  #0ff,
               4px 5px 6px  #00f,
               0px 0px 10px #444,
               0px 0px 20px #844,
               0px 0px 30px #a44,
               0px 0px 40px #f44;
}

#text4 {
  position: absolute;
  top: 200px;
  right: 200px;
  font-size: 48pt;
  text-shadow: 0px 1px 6px  #fff,
               2px 4px 4px  #0ff,
               4px 5px 6px  #00f,
               0px 0px 10px #000,
               0px 0px 20px #448,
               0px 0px 30px #a4a,
               0px 0px 40px #fff;
  -webkit-transform: rotate(-90deg);
  transform: rotate(-90deg);
}
```

```
#text5 {
  position: absolute;
  left: 0px;
  font-size: 48pt;
  text-shadow: 2px 4px 5px #00f;
  -webkit-transform: rotate(-10deg);
 transform: rotate(-10deg);
}

#text6 {
  float: left;
  font-size: 48pt;
  text-shadow: 2px 4px 5px #f00;
  -webkit-transform: rotate(-170deg);
  transform: rotate(-170deg);
}

/* 'transform' is explained later */
#text1:hover, #text2:hover, #text3:hover,
#text4:hover, #text5:hover, #text6:hover {
-webkit-transform : scale(2) rotate(-45deg);
transform : scale(2) rotate(-45deg);
}
```

The first selector in Listing 3.2 specifies a font-size of 24 and a text-shadow that renders text with a blue background (represented by the hexadecimal value #00f). The attribute text-shadow specifies (from left to right) the x-coordinate, the y-coordinate, the blur radius, and the color of the shadow. The second selector specifies a font-size of 32 and a red shadow background (#f00). The third selector creates a richer visual effect by specifying multiple components in the text-shadow property, which were chosen by experimenting with effects that are possible with different values in the various components.

The final CSS3 selector creates an animation effect whenever users hover over any of the six text strings, and the details of the animation will be deferred until later in this chapter.

One other detail pertains to the legibility of text strings when you render them with a text shadow effect. Sometimes you can create a slightly sharper effect by using the following property/value combination in a CSS selector:

```
text-shadow:0 0 1px transparent;
```

Figure 3.1 displays the result of matching the selectors in the CSS stylesheet TextShadow1.css with the HTML <div> elements in the HTML page TextShadow1.html. The landscape-mode screenshot is taken from an Android application (based on the code in Listing 3.1 and Listing 3.2) running on a Nexus S 4G (Android ICS) smart phone.

FIGURE 3.1 CSS3 Text Shadow Effects.

CSS3 and Box Shadow Effects

You can also apply a shadow effect to a box that encloses a text string, which can be effective in terms of drawing attention to specific parts of a Web page. However, the same caveat regarding over-use applies to box shadows.

The HTML page `BoxShadow1.html` and `BoxShadow1.css` are not shown here but they are available on the DVD, and together they render a box shadow effect.

The key property is the `box-shadow` property, as shown here in bold for Mozilla, WebKit, and the non-prefixed property:

```
#box1 {
  position:relative;top:10px;
  width: 50%;
  height: 30px;
  font-size: 20px;
  -moz-box-shadow: 10px 10px 5px #800;
  -webkit-box-shadow: 10px 10px 5px #800;
  box-shadow: 10px 10px 5px #800;
```

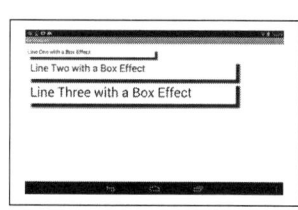

Figure 3.2 displays a landscape-mode screen-shot taken from a Nexus 7 2 with Android Jelly-Bean 4.3.

FIGURE 3.2 CSS3 Box Shadow Effect on a Sprint Nexus with Android ICS.

CSS3 and Rounded Corners

Web developers have waited a long time for rounded corners in CSS, and CSS3 makes it very easy to render boxes with rounded corners. Listing 3.3 displays the contents of the HTML page `RoundedCorners1.html` that renders text strings in boxes with rounded corners, and Listing 3.4 displays the CSS file `RoundedCorners1.css`.

LISTING 3.3 RoundedCorners1.html

```
<!DOCTYPE html>
<html lang="en">
<head>
  <link href="RoundedCorners1.css" rel="stylesheet" type="text/
css">
</head>
<body>
  <div id="outer">
    <a href="#" class="anchor">Text Inside a Rounded Rectangle</a>
  </div>
  <div id="text1">Line One of Text with a Shadow Effect</div>
  <div id="text2">Line Two of Text with a Shadow Effect</div>
</body>
</html>
```

Listing 3.3 contains a reference to the CSS stylesheet `Rounded-Corners1.css` that contains three CSS selectors that match the elements whose `id` attribute has value `anchor`, `text1`, and `text2`, respectively. The

CSS selectors defined in `RoundedCorners1.css` create visual effects, and as you will see, the `hover` pseudo-selector enables you to create animation effects.

LISTING 3.4 RoundedCorners1.css

```
a.anchor:hover {
background: #00F;
}

a.anchor {
background: #FF0;
font-size: 24px;
font-weight: bold;
padding: 4px 4px;
color: rgba(255,0,0,0.8);
text-shadow: 0 1px 1px rgba(0,0,0,0.4);
-webkit-transition: all 2.0s ease;
transition: all 2.0s ease;
-webkit-border-radius: 8px;
border-radius: 8px;
}
```

Listing 3.4 contains the selector `a.anchor:hover` that changes the text color from yellow (`#FF0`) to blue (`#00F`) during a two-second interval whenever users hover over any anchor element with their mouse.

The selector `a.anchor` contains various attributes that specify the dimensions of the box that encloses the text in the `<a>` element, along with two new pairs of attributes. The first pair specifies the `transition` attribute (and a `WebKit`-specific prefix), which we will discuss later in this chapter. The second pair specifies the `border-radius` attribute (and the `WebKit`-specific

attribute) whose value is `8px`, which determines the radius (in pixels) of the rounded corners of the box that encloses the text in the `<a>` element. The last two selectors are identical to the selectors in Listing 3.1.

Figure 3.3 displays the result of matching the selectors that are defined in the CSS stylesheet `RoundedCorners1.css` with elements in the HTML page `RoundedCorners1.html` taken from a Nexus 7 2 with Android JellyBean 4.3.

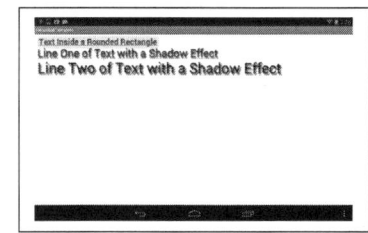

FIGURE 3.3 CSS3 Rounded Corners Effect on a Nexus 7 2 Android JellyBean 4.3.

CSS3 GRADIENTS

CSS3 supports linear gradients and radial gradients, which enable you to create gradient effects that are as visually rich as gradients in other technologies such as SVG. The code samples in this section illustrate how to define linear gradients in CSS3 and then match them to HTML elements.

Linear Gradients

CSS3 linear gradients require you to specify one or more "color stops," each of which specifies a start color, an end color, and a rendering pattern. Webkit-based browsers support the following syntax to define a linear gradient:

- a start point
- an end point
- a start color using from()
- zero or more color-stops
- an end color using to()

A start point can be specified as an (x,y) pair of numbers or percentages. For example, the pair (100,25%) specifies the point that is 100 pixels to the right of the origin and 25% of the way down from the top of the pattern. Recall that the origin is located in the upper-left corner of the screen.

Listing 3.5 displays the contents of LinearGradient1.html and Listing 3.6 displays the contents of LinearGradient1.css, which illustrate how to use linear gradients with text strings that are enclosed in <p> elements and an <h3> element.

LISTING 3.5 LinearGradient1.html

```
<!doctype html>
<html lang="en">
<head>
  <title>CSS Linear Gradient Example</title>
  <meta charset="utf-8" />
  <link href="LinearGradient1.css" rel="stylesheet" type="text/
css">
</head>

<body>
  <div id="outer">
    <p id="line1">line 1 with a linear gradient</p>
    <p id="line2">line 2 with a linear gradient</p>
    <p id="line3">line 3 with a linear gradient</p>
    <p id="line4">line 4 with a linear gradient</p>
    <p id="outline">line 5 with Shadow Outline</p>
    <h3><a href="#">A Line of Gradient Text</a></h3>
  </div>
</body>
</html>
```

Listing 3.5 is a simple Web page containing four <p> elements and one <h3> element. Listing 3.5 also references the CSS stylesheet LinearGradient1.css that contains CSS selectors that match the four <p> elements and the <h3> element in Listing 3.5.

LISTING 3.6 LinearGradient1.css

```
#line1 {
width: 50%;
```

```
font-size: 32px;
background-image: -webkit-gradient(linear, 0% 0%, 0% 100%,
                                    from(#fff), to(#f00));
background-image: -gradient(linear, 0% 0%, 0% 100%,
                            from(#fff), to(#f00));
-webkit-border-radius: 4px;
border-radius: 4px;
}

#line2 {
width: 50%;
font-size: 32px;
background-image: -webkit-gradient(linear, 100% 0%, 0% 100%,
                                    from(#fff), to(#ff0));
background-image: -gradient(linear, 100% 0%, 0% 100%,
                            from(#fff), to(#ff0));
-webkit-border-radius: 4px;
border-radius: 4px;
}

#line3 {
width: 50%;
font-size: 32px;
background-image: -webkit-gradient(linear, 0% 0%, 0% 100%,
                                    from(#f00), to(#00f));
background-image: -gradient(linear, 0% 0%, 0% 100%,
                            from(#f00), to(#00f));
-webkit-border-radius: 4px;
border-radius: 4px;
}

#line4 {
width: 50%;
font-size: 32px;
background-image: -webkit-gradient(linear, 100% 0%, 0% 100%,
                                    from(#f00), to(#00f));
background-image: -gradient(linear, 100% 0%, 0% 100%,
                            from(#f00), to(#00f));
-webkit-border-radius: 4px;
border-radius: 4px;
}

#outline {
font-size: 2.0em;
font-weight: bold;
color: #fff;
text-shadow: 1px 1px 1px rgba(0,0,0,0.5);
}

h3 {
width: 50%;
position: relative;
margin-top: 0;
font-size: 32px;
font-family: helvetica, ariel;
}
```

```
h3 a {
position: relative;
color: red;
text-decoration: none;
-webkit-mask-image:  -webkit-gradient(linear, left top, left bottom,
                        from(rgba(0,0,0,1)),
                        color-stop(50%, rgba(0,0,0,0.5)),
                        to(rgba(0,0,0,0))));
}

h3:after {
content:"This is a Line of Gradient Text";
color: blue;
}
```

The first selector in Listing 3.6 specifies a `font-size` of 32 for text, a `border-radius` of 4 (which renders rounded corners), and a linear gradient that varies from white to blue, as shown here:

```
#line1 {
width: 50%;
font-size: 32px;
background-image: -webkit-gradient(linear, 0% 0%, 0% 100%,
                        from(#fff), to(#f00));
background-image: -gradient(linear, 0% 0%, 0% 100%,
                        from(#fff), to(#f00));
-webkit-border-radius: 4px;
border-radius: 4px;
}
```

As you can see, the first selector contains two attributes with a `-webkit-` prefix and two standard attributes without this prefix. Since the next three selectors in Listing 3.6 are similar to the first selector, we will not discuss their content.

The next CSS selector creates a text outline with a nice shadow effect by rendering the text in white with a thin black shadow, as shown here:

```
color: #fff;
text-shadow: 1px 1px 1px rgba(0,0,0,0.5);
```

The final portion of Listing 3.6 contains three selectors that affect the rendering of the `<h3>` element and its embedded `<a>` element: the h3 selector specifies the width and font size; the h3 selector specifies a linear gradient; and the h3:after selector specifies the text string to display. Other attributes are specified, but these are the main attributes for these selectors.

Figure 3.4 displays the result of matching the selectors in the CSS stylesheet `LinearGradient1.css` to the HTML page `LinearGradient1.html` taken from a Nexus 7 2 with Android JellyBean 4.3.

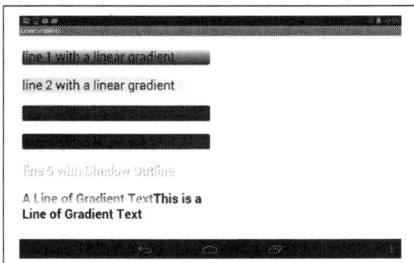

FIGURE 3.4 CSS3 Linear Gradient Effect on a Nexus 7 2 Android JellyBean 4.3.

CSS3 2D TRANSFORMS

In addition to transitions, CSS3 supports a number of transforms that you can apply to 2D shapes and also to JPG files. The transforms `scale`, `rotate`, `skew`, `translate`, `matrix`, and `perspective` in CSS3 might be familiar to you from other programming languages. Since the `skew` transform will soon be deprecated, the `skewX` and `skewY` transforms are recommended instead of the `skew` transform.

The following sections contain code samples that illustrate how to apply the first four CSS3 transforms to a set of JPG files. The animation effects occur when users hover over any of the JPG files; moreover, you can create "partial" animation effects by moving your mouse quickly between adjacent JPG files.

Listing 3.7 displays the contents of `Scale1.html` and Listing 3.8 displays the contents of `Scale1.css`, which illustrate how to scale JPG files to create a "hover box" image gallery.

LISTING 3.7 Scale1.html

```
<!DOCTYPE html>
<html lang="en">
<head>
  <title>CSS Scale Transform Example</title>
  <meta charset="utf-8" />
  <link href="Scale1.css" rel="stylesheet" type="text/css">
</head>

<body>
  <header>
  <h1>Hover Over any of the Images:</h1>
  </header>

  <div id="outer">
    <img src="sample1.png" class="scaled" width="150" height="150"/>
    <img src="sample2.png" class="scaled" width="150" height="150"/>
    <img src="sample1.png" class="scaled" width="150" height="150"/>
    <img src="sample2.png" class="scaled" width="150" height="150"/>
  </div>
</body>
</html>
```

Listing 3.7 references the CSS stylesheet `Scale1.css` (which contains selectors for creating scaled effects) and four HTML `<img>` elements that references the JPG files `sample1.png` and `sample2.pngg`. The remainder of Listing 3.7 is straightforward, with simple boilerplate text and HTML elements.

LISTING 3.8 Scale1.css

```
#outer {
float: left;
position: relative; top: 50px; left: 50px;
}

img {
-webkit-transition: -webkit-transform 1.0s ease;
transition: transform 1.0s ease;
}

img.scaled {
  -webkit-box-shadow: 10px 10px 5px #800;
  box-shadow: 10px 10px 5px #800;
}

img.scaled:hover {
-webkit-transform : scale(2);
transform : scale(2);
}
```

The `img` selector in Listing 3.8 contains specifies a `transition` property that applies a `transform` effect that occurs during a one-second interval using the `ease` function, as shown here:

```
transition: transform 1.0s ease;
```

Next, the selector `img.scaled` specifies a `box-shadow` property that creates a reddish shadow effect (which you saw earlier in this chapter), as shown here:

```
img.scaled {
  -webkit-box-shadow: 10px 10px 5px #800;
  box-shadow: 10px 10px 5px #800;
}
```

Finally, the selector `img.scaled:hover` specifies a `transform` attribute that uses the `scale()` function in order to double the size of the associated JPG file whenever users hover over any of the `<img>` elements with their mouse, as shown here:

```
transform : scale(2);
```

Because the `img` selector specifies a one-second interval using an `ease` function, the scaling effect will last for one second. Experiment with different values for the CSS3 `scale()` function and also a different value for the time interval to create the animation effects that suit your needs.

Another point to remember is that you can scale both horizontally and vertically:

```
img {
-webkit-transition: -webkit-transform 1.0s ease;
transition: transform 1.0s ease;
}

img.mystyle:hover {
-webkit-transform : scaleX(1.5) scaleY(0.5);
transform : scaleX(1.5) scaleY(0.5);
}
```

Figure 3.5 displays the result of matching the selectors in the CSS stylesheet `Scale1.css` to the HTML page `Scale1.html`. The landscape-mode screenshot is taken from an Android application (based on the code in Listing 3.7 and Listing 3.8) running on a Nexus S 4G smart phone with Android ICS.

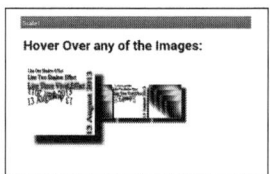

FIGURE 3.5 CSS3-based Scaling Effect on JPG Files.

Rotate Transforms

The CSS3 `transform` attribute allows you to specify the `rotate()` function in order to create scaling effects, and its syntax looks like this:

```
rotate(someValue);
```

You can replace `someValue` with any number. When `someValue` is positive, the rotation is clockwise; when `someValue` is negative, the rotation is counter clockwise; and when `someValue` is zero, there is no rotation effect. In all cases, the initial position for the rotation effect is the positive horizontal axis.

The HTML5 Web page `Rotate1.html` and the CSS stylesheet `Rotate1.css` on the DVD illustrate how to create rotation effects, a sample of which is shown here:

```
img.imageL:hover {
-webkit-transform : scale(2) rotate(-45deg);
transform : scale(2) rotate(-45deg);
}
```

The `img` selector that specifies a `transition` attribute that creates an animation effect during a one-second interval using the `ease` timing function, as shown here:

```
transition: transform 1.0s ease;
```

The CSS3 transform attribute allows you to specify the `skewX()` and the `skewY()` function in order to create skewing effects, and the syntax looks like this:

```
skewX(xAngle);
skewY(yAngle);
```

You can replace xAngle and yAngle with any number. When xAngle and yAngle are positive, the skew effect is clockwise; when xAngle and yAngle are negative, the skew effect is counter clockwise; and when xAngle and yAngle are zero, there is no skew effect. In all cases, the initial position for the skew effect is the positive horizontal axis.

The HTML5 Web page Skew1.html and the CSS stylesheet Skew1. css are on the DVD, and they illustrate how to create skew effects. The CSS stylesheet contains the img selector specifies a transition attribute that creates an animation effect during a one-second interval using the ease timing function, as shown here:

```
transition: transform 1.0s ease;
```

There are also the four selectors img.skewed1, img.skewed2, img. skewed3, and img.skewed4 that create background shadow effects with darker shades of red, yellow, green, and blue, respectively (all of which you have seen in earlier code samples).

The selector img.skewed1:hover specifies a transform attribute that performs a skew effect whenever users hover over the first <img> element with their mouse, as shown here:

```
transform : scale(2) skewX(-10deg) skewY(-30deg);
```

The other three CSS3 selectors also use a combination of the CSS functions skew() and scale() to create distinct visual effects. Notice that the fourth hover selector also sets the opacity property to 0.5, which takes place in parallel with the other effects in this selector.

Figure 3.6 displays the result of matching the selectors in the CSS stylesheet Skew1. css to the elements in the HTML page Skew1.html. The landscape-mode screenshot is taken from an Android application running on a Nexus S 4G smart phone with Android ICS.

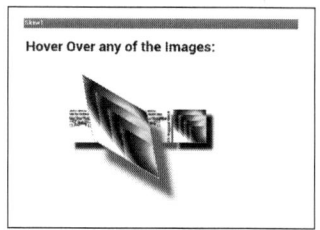

FIGURE 3.6 CSS3-based Skew Effects on JPG Files.

The CSS3 transform attribute allows you to specify the translate() function in order to create an effect that involves a horizontal and/or vertical "shift" of an element, and its syntax looks like this:

```
translate(xDirection, yDirection);
```

The translation is in relation to the origin, which is the upper-left corner of the screen. Thus, positive values for xDirection and yDirection produce a shift toward the right and a shift downward, respectively, whereas negative values for xDirection and yDirection produce a shift toward the left and a shift upward; zero values for xDirection and yDirection do not cause any translation effect.

The Web page `Translate1.html` and the CSS stylesheet `Translate1.css` on the DVD illustrate how to apply a translation effect to a JPG file.

```
img.trans2:hover {
-webkit-transform : scale(0.5) translate(-50px, -50px);
transform : scale(0.5) translate(-50px, -50px);
}
```

The CSS stylesheet contains the `img` selector that specifies a transform effect during a one-second interval using the `ease` timing function, as shown here:

```
transition: transform 1.0s ease;
```

The four selectors, `img.trans1`, `img.trans2`, `img.trans3`, and `img.trans4`, create background shadow effects with darker shades of red, yellow, green, and blue, respectively, just as you saw in the previous section.

The selector `img.trans1:hover` specifies a `transform` attribute that performs a scale effect and a translation effect whenever users hover over the first `<img>` element with their mouse, as shown here:

```
-webkit-transform : scale(2) translate(100px, 50px);
transform : scale(2) translate(100px, 50px);
```

Figure 3.7 displays the result of matching the selectors defined in the CSS3 stylesheet `Translate1.css` to the elements in the HTML page `Translate1.html`. The landscape-mode screenshot is taken from an Android application running on a Nexus S 4G smart phone with Android ICS.

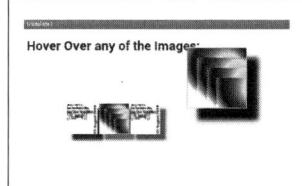

FIGURE 3.7 JPG Files with CSS3 Scale and Translate Effects.

PREBUILT CSS STYLESHEETS: `RESET.CSS` AND `NORMALIZE.CSS`

You can create a custom CSS stylesheet for setting properties of HTML elements in your HTML Web pages, but before doing so, it's worth your time to explore two popular CSS stylesheets that can perform this task for you.

The first popular CSS stylesheet (written by Eric Meyer) is `reset.css`, and its homepage is here:

http://meyerweb.com/eric/tools/css/reset/

The second popular CSS stylesheet is `normalize.css` and its homepage is here:

http://necolas.github.io/normalize.css/

You can also install `normalize.css` from the command line as follows:

```
bower install -save normalize-css
```

According to the `normalize.css` homepage:

"[`normalize.css`] makes browsers render all elements more consistently and in line with modern standards. It precisely targets only the styles that need normalizing."

If you are wondering how to decide which of these CSS stylesheets to use (or if you actually even need to use either one of them) in an HTML Web page, a useful link that addresses this question is here:

http://www.cssreset.com/which-css-reset-should-i-use/

SUMMARY

This chapter showed you how to create graphics effects, shadow effects, and how to use CSS3 transforms in CSS3. You learned how to create animation effects that you can apply to HTML elements, and you saw how to define CSS3 selectors to do the following:

- render rounded rectangles
- create shadow effects for text and 2D shapes
- create linear gradients
- use the methods `translate()`, `rotate()`, `skew()`, and `scale()`
- create CSS3-based animation effects

META TAGS AND MEDIA QUERIES

This chapter covers meta tags, CSS3 Media Queries, and CSS frameworks for developing HTML5 mobile applications. The approach that you adopt for developing HTML5 mobile applications probably depends on various factors (project scope and specific requirements) that often involve trade-offs. The spectrum of available techniques, ranging from "pure" JavaScript (more work for you, but a smaller code footprint) to frameworks (larger codebase, but many details are handled for you), affords a range of choices for your HTML5 Web application development.

The first part of this chapter discusses generic meta tags for mobile devices, along with iOS-specific and Android-specific meta tags. You will also learn how to use "pure" JavaScript in order to detect device orientation (portrait or landscape) and property values (such as the screen width and height) and then update those properties appropriately.

The second part of this chapter discusses CSS3 Media Queries, which enable you to detect some characteristics of a device, and render an HTML5 Web page based on those device characteristics. You'll see examples of using CSS3 media queries to change the layout of a Web page based on the orientation of a mobile device.

THE VIEWPORT META TAG

Web pages are rendered in a "virtual page," and the screen is a window into that page. The `viewport` meta tag sets the dimensions of this virtual page. In addition, the `viewport` meta tag controls scaling of the browser window in iOS, Android, WebOS, Opera Mini, Opera Mobile, and Blackberry. The `viewport` meta tag supports the following attributes:

- width: The width of the viewport in pixels (the default is 980) can be between 200 and 10,000.

- height: The height of the viewport in pixels. The default is calculated based on the width and the aspect ratio of the device, and it can be between 223 and 10,000.
- initial-scale: The initial "zoom factor" of an application, which users can then scale in and out from that initial value.
- minimum-scale: The minimum scale value of the viewport (the default is 0.25), which can be between 0 and 10.0.
- maximum-scale: The maximum scale value of the viewport (the default is 1.6), which can be between 0 and 10.0.
- user-scalable: You can specify whether or not users can zoom in and out of an application (the default is "yes."). Set the value to "no" to prevent scaling.

In addition, you can set more than one viewport option in your meta tag by separating them with commas, as shown here:

```
<meta name="viewport" content="width=device-width, user-scalable=no">
```

The `target-densitydpi` property (specified in the `viewport` meta tag) has been deprecated (and actually removed from WebKit), so it's inadvisable to use this property in order to specify low, medium, or high dpi values in Android-based mobile applications.

You can also use the `viewport` tag in order to prevent users from zooming or panning in a mobile application. An example is here:

```
<meta name="viewport"
content="width=device-width; initial-scale=1.0; maximum-scale=1.0;
user-scalable=0;" />
```

The iOS platform supports the `viewpoint` meta tag as well as iOS-specific meta tags, some of which are described here:

*http://developer.apple.com/library/safari/documentation/
appleapplications/reference/SafariHTMLRef/Articles/MetaTags.html#//
apple_ref/doc/uid/TP40008193-SW1*

The next portion of this chapter discusses the `@import` statement for importing a CSS stylesheet into another CSS stylesheet, followed by a discussion of media queries.

THE @IMPORT STATEMENT IN CSS3

The `@import` statement conveniently enables you to import a CSS stylesheet into another stylesheet. For example, suppose that you want to import the CSS stylesheet `basic.css` into the CSS stylesheet `extended.css`, both of which are in the same directory on the filesystem. You can do so with the following code snippet:

```
@import basic.css
```

You can also import a CSS stylesheet that is available on the Internet instead of the file system, as shown here:

```
@import url(http://www.princexml.com/fonts/larabie/index.css) all;
```

The next section discusses two important considerations to keep in mind when you use the @import statement in CSS stylesheets.

Modularization and Performance

Although the @import statement can be very convenient, there are two points to consider when you use the use this statement. First, the @import statement can help you modularize your CSS stylesheets, but keep in mind that you need to watch for overriding properties when it's not your intention to do so. Second, there can also be a performance penalty. One popular technique for mitigating the performance degradation is to use a tool that merges files together and then compresses the single concatenated file. This approach reduces the number of HTTP requests and also the total file size that is sent to a Web page.

SCOPED CSS STYLESHEETS (EXPERIMENTAL)

The latest version of Google Chromium (currently version 29) supports the <style scoped> feature, which is a new HTML5 feature called scoped stylesheets. This feature limits the scope of style rules to a subtree in a Web page, where the root of the subtree is the *parent* of an element that matches the CSS selector.

The following Web page illustrates how to use the <style scoped> feature:

```
<html>
<body>
  <div>div1 and <p>paragraph1</p></div>
    <div>
      <style scoped>
        div  { color: blue; }
        p    { color: red; }
      </style>
      <div>div2 and <p>paragraph2</p></div>
  <div>div3 and <p>paragraph3</p></div>
</body>
</html>
```

http://updates.html5rocks.com/2012/03/A-New-Experimental-Feature-style-scoped

WHAT ARE CSS3 MEDIA QUERIES?

CSS3 media queries extend the capability of an older CSS specification known as media types, which assigned browsers to high-level categories such as screen, handheld, or print in order to re-style a Web page's printed output.

CSS 2.1 introduced the concept of media queries, which enable you to conditionally include alternative style sheets for print, screen, and so forth. The media types specification details describes 10 media types, but browsers only support a few of them (such as screen and print).

For example, the following CSS 2.1 media queries conditionally load CSS stylesheets based on the value of the media attribute:

```
<link rel="stylesheet" type="text/css"
      href="main.css" media="screen" />
<link rel="stylesheet" type="text/css"
      href="print.css" media="print" />
```

The CSS3 media queries module extends the idea of media types introduced in CSS 2.1, and all modern desktop and major mobile browsers support CSS3-based media queries.

CSS3 media queries give you the ability to determine some of the physical characteristics of a device visiting a site. In a sense, CSS3 media queries are the counterpart to feature detection. For example, the following CSS3 media query combines two conditions as the conditional logic for loading a CSS stylesheet:

```
<link rel="stylesheet"
      media="screen and (min-width: 800px)" href="main.css" />
```

You can also use media queries inline in CSS using @media directives in order to conditionally style various HTML elements, as illustrated in the following example:

```
@media screen and (min-width: 320px) {
   body {
     background-color: #ff0000;
   }
}

@media screen and (min-width: 480px) {
   body {
     background-color: #0000ff;
   }
}
```

This section contains an assortment of CSS3 media queries, which are very useful logical expressions that enable you to detect mobile applications on devices with differing physical attributes and orientation. For example, with CSS3 media queries you can change the dimensions and layout of your applications so that they render appropriately on smart phones as well as tablets.

Specifically, you can use CSS3 media queries in order to determine the following characteristics of a device:

- browser window width and height
- device width and height
- orientation (landscape or portrait)
- aspect ratio
- device aspect ratio
- resolution

CSS3 media queries are Boolean expressions that contain one or more "simple terms" (connected with and or or) that evaluate to true or false. Thus, CSS3 media queries represent conditional logic that evaluates to either true or false.

As an example, the following link element loads the CSS stylesheet mystuff.css only if the device is a screen and the maximum width of the device is 480px:

```
<link rel="stylesheet" type="text/css"
      media="screen and (max-device-width: 480px)" href="mystuff.css"/>
```

The preceding link contains a media attribute that specifies two components: a media type of screen and a query that specifies a max-device-width whose value is 480px. The supported values for media in CSS3 media queries are braille, embossed, handheld, print, projection, screen, speech, tty, and tv.

The next CSS3 media query checks the media type, the maximum device width, and the resolution of a device:

```
@media screen and (max-device-width: 480px) and (resolution: 160dpi) {
  #innerDiv {
    float: none;
  }
}
```

If the CSS3 media query in the preceding code snippet evaluates to true, then the nested CSS selector will match the HTML element whose id attribute has the value innerDiv, and its float property will be set to none on any device whose maximum screen width is 480px. As you can see, it's possible to create compact CSS3 media queries that contain non-trivial logic, which is obviously very useful because CSS3 does not have any if/then/else construct that is available in other programming languages.

The next CSS3 media query tests the media type, the minimum device width, and the resolution of a device:

```
@media screen and (min-device-width: 481px) and (resolution: 160dpi) {
  #innerDiv {
    float: left;
  }
}
```

In the preceding CSS3 selector, the HTML element whose `id` attribute has the value `innerDiv` will have a `float` property whose value is left on any device whose minimum screen width is `481px`.

The next CSS3 media query sets the width of `div` elements to `100px` if the screen width is between `321` and `480`:

```
@media screen and (min-width: 321px) and (max-width: 480px) {
    div { width: 100px; }
}
```

In the following code snippet, `myphone.css` would apply to devices that the browser considers "handheld" or devices with the screen width at most `320px`:

```
<link rel="stylesheet" media="handheld, only screen and (max-device-
width: 320px)" href="myphone.css">
```

Note: The use of the "only" keyword in media queries causes non CSS3-compliant browsers to ignore the rule. As another example, the following `<link>` loads a CSS stylesheet for screen sizes between `641px` and `800px`:

```
<link rel="stylesheet" media="only screen and (min-width: 641px)
and (max-width: 800px)" href="wide.css">
```

Media queries can be included in inline `<style>` tags, as shown in this query, which is for all media types in `portrait` mode:

```
<style> @media only all and (orientation: portrait) { ... } </
style>
```

Now that you have a basic understanding of the sorts of things that you can do with `CSS3 Media Queries`, you can follow the code in the next section, which contains an HTML5 Web page and a CSS3 stylesheet that illustrate how to handle a change of orientation of a mobile device.

DETECTING SCREEN RESOLUTION WITH CSS3 MEDIA QUERIES

Currently, there are few CSS3 Media Queries that are specific to Android devices or for iOS devices. Fortunately, you can use CSS3 Media Queries with conditional logic based on different screen sizes or different screen resolutions, some of which are specific to Android devices and to iOS devices. You can determine a specific resolution by using the resolution keyword to test for various dots per inch (`dpi`). You can also specify the min- and max- prefixes to show stylesheets for low-res and high-res machines.

4G iPhone and iPod touches use a high-definition Retina display. You can use a WebKit keyword to test for its presence:

```
-webkit-min-device-pixel-ratio
```

To display only to Retina devices, you would use the following conditional logic:

```
only screen and (-webkit-min-device-pixel-ratio: 2)
```

DETECTING SCREEN ORIENTATION WITH CSS3 MEDIA QUERIES

The CSS3 media queries in this section provide a simple example of the capabilities of CSS3 media queries.

Listing 4.1 and 4.2 display the contents of the stylesheet CSS3Medi-aQuery1.css and the HTML5 Web page CSS3MediaQuery1.html that illustrate how to change the size of two images when users rotate their mobile device.

LISTING 4.1 CSS3MediaQuery1.css

```
@media all and (orientation: portrait) {
  #img1, #img2 {
  float: left;
  width:120px;
  height:300px;
  }
}

@media all and (orientation: landscape) {
  #img1, #img2 {
  float: left;
  width:200px;
  height:200px;
  }
}
```

The code in Listing 4.1 is straightforward: the first selector specifies values for the float, width, and height properties of two JPG files when your mobile device is in portrait mode; the second selector specifies different values for the width and height properties of the two JPG files when your device is in landscape mode.

LISTING 4.2 CSS3MediaQuery1.html

```
<!DOCTYPE html>
<html lang="en">
<head>
  <meta charset="utf-8" >
  <title>CSS3 Media Query </title>
  <link href="CSS3MediaQuery1.css" rel="stylesheet" type="text/css">
</head>

<body>
  <header>
   <h2>Rotate Your Device:</h2>
  </header>
```

```
<div id="outer">
  <div id="one">
    <img id="img1" src="sample1.png" />
  </div>
  <div id="two">
    <img id="img2" src="sample2.png" />
  </div>
</div>
</body>
</html>
```

FIGURE 4.1 CSS3 Media Query on a Sprint Nexus S 4G Smart Phone with Android ICS.

Listing 4.2 references the CSS stylesheet CSS3Me-diaQuery1.css in Listing 4.1 in order to apply CSS selectors to the JPG files in the <body> element. Next, the HTML <body> element contains two HTML <div> elements whose id attributes have the values img1 and img2 that are referenced in the corresponding CSS selectors.

Figure 4.1 displays the result of rendering the HTML page CSS3MediaQuery.html in landscape mode on a Sprint Nexus S 4G smart phone with Android ICS.

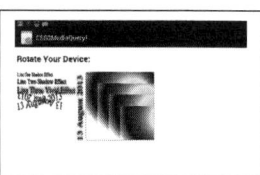

FIGURE 4.2 CSS3 Media Query on a Sprint Nexus S 4G Smart Phone with Android ICS.

Figure 4.2 displays the result of rendering the HTML page CSS3MediaQuery.html in landscape mode.

DETECTING ORIENTATION WITH SIMPLE JAVASCRIPT

Earlier in this chapter, you saw how to use CSS3 media queries in order to detect an orientation change of a mobile device. However, keep in mind that it's also possible to do the same thing with simple JavaScript code, so you are not "forced" to use CSS3 media queries.

Listing 4.3 displays the contents of the Web page CSS3Orienta-tionJS1.html that illustrates how to use standard JavaScript in order to change the size of two images when users rotate their mobile device.

LISTING 4.3 CSS3OrientationJS1.html

```
<!DOCTYPE html>
<html lang="en">
<head>
  <meta charset="utf-8" >
  <title>CSS3 and Orientation with JS</title>

  <style>
  #img1, #img2 {
     float: left;
     width:120px;height:300px;
  }
  </style>
```

```
<script>
  function init() {
    // Event listener to determine device orientation
    window.onresize = function() { updateOrientation(); }
  }

  function updateOrientation() {
    var orientation = window.orientation;

    switch(orientation) {
      case 0: /* portrait mode */
          document.getElementById("img1").style.width  = "120px";
          document.getElementById("img1").style.height = "300px";
          document.getElementById("img2").style.width  = "120px";
          document.getElementById("img2").style.height = "300px";
          break;

      case 90: /* landscape (screen turned to the left) */
          document.getElementById("img1").style.width  = "200px";
          document.getElementById("img1").style.height = "200px";
          document.getElementById("img2").style.width  = "200px";
          document.getElementById("img2").style.height = "200px";
          break;

      case -90: /* landscape (screen turned to the right) */
          document.getElementById("img1").style.width  = "200px";
          document.getElementById("img1").style.height = "200px";
          document.getElementById("img2").style.width  = "200px";
          document.getElementById("img2").style.height = "200px";
          break;
    }
  }
</script>
</head>

<body onload="init()">
  <header>
   <h2>Rotate Your Device:</h2>
  </header>

  <div id="outer">
    <div id="one">
      <img id="img1" src="sample1.png" />
    </div>
    <div id="two">
      <img id="img2" src="sample2.png" />
    </div>
  </div>
</body>
</html>
```

As you can see, there is much more code in Listing 4.3 compared to Listing 4.2. In essence, the code uses the value of the variable `window.orientation` in order to detect four different orientations of your mobile device, and in each of those four cases, the dimensions of the JPG files are updated with the following type of code:

```
document.getElementById("img1").style.width  = "120px";
document.getElementById("img1").style.height = "300px";
```

Although this is a very simple example, hopefully this code gives you an appreciation for the capabilities of CSS3 media queries.

DETECTING DEVICE ORIENTATION IN 3D USING JAVASCRIPT

The previous section showed you how to determine the orientation of a device in terms of whether it's in portrait mode or landscape mode. In addition, you can determine the position of a device in 3D.

There are three types of changes in the 3D position of a device: up and down (z axis), left and right (y axis), and clockwise and counter-clockwise (x axis). These changes are measured with an accelerometer, and you can check their current values in the deviceorientation event on the window object. This event fires whenever the mobile device moves, and it returns an object with orientation-related properties.

The JavaScript code looks like the following:

```
window.addEventListener('deviceorientation',function (o) {
  console.log(o.alpha,o.beta,o.gamma);
}, false);
```

The three properties alpha, beta, and gamma provide the rotation angle (in degrees, not radians) in the z, x, and y axes, respectively. Keep in mind that the z axis is the vertical axis (positive is upward), the x axis points toward you (negative is away from you), and the y axis is a left-to-right horizontal axis (toward the right is positive).

The allowable values for these three properties are as follows:

```
alpha: 0 to 360 (clockwise)
beta:  -180 to 180 (toward you/away from you)
gamma: -90 to 90  (left to right)
```

If you want more details regarding the orientation of a device, you can use the accelerometer to obtain more precise information. An example of using Apache Cordova to access information from the accelerometer is discussed in Chapter 5.

DETECTING SCREEN WIDTH AND HEIGHT

The window object supports a resize event that you can use for determining the width and height of the screen, which in turn enables you to modify other effects in HTML5 Web pages. Listing 4.4 displays the contents of ResizeBorder1.html that illustrates how to maintain the same blue border regardless of the screen size or screen orientation.

LISTING 4.4 ResizeBorder1.html

```
<!DOCTYPE html>
<html lang="en">
<head>
  <meta charset="utf-8" >
  <title>Resizing the Window</title>

  <style>
    * {
      margin:0px; padding:0;
    }

    #outer {
      width: 400px; height: 300px;
      border: 10px solid blue;
    }
  </style>

  <link rel="stylesheet"
   href="http://code.jquery.com/mobile/1.1.0/jquery.mobile-
1.1.0.min.css" />
  <script
    src="http://code.jquery.com/jquery-2.0.0b1.js">
  </script>
  <script
    src="http://code.jquery.com/jquery-migrate-1.1.0.js">
  </script>
  <script
src="http://code.jquery.com/mobile/1.1.0/jquery.mobile-1.1.0.min.js">
  </script>
</head>

<body onload="resizeBorder();">
  <div id="outer">
  </div>

  <script>
    // borderWidth equals 'border' in the CSS selector above
    var borderWidth = 10;

    window.onresize = function() { resizeBorder(); }

    function resizeBorder() {
      // do the following if the screen has been resized:
      var rescaledScreenWidth  = document.documentElement.clientWidth;
      var rescaledScreenHeight = document.documentElement.clientHeight;

      $("#outer").css('width',  rescaledScreenWidth-2*borderWidth);
      $("#outer").css('height', rescaledScreenHeight-2*borderWidth);
    }
  </script>
</body>
</html>
```

Listing 4.4 contains a `<style>` element whose first selector sets the `padding` and `margin` to 0px for all elements in the Web page. The second selector specifies a blue border of 10px. When you load this Web page into a border, and whenever you resize the browser, the JavaScript function re-sizeBorder() is executed. This JavaScript function obtains the current width and height of the browser with this code snippet:

```
var rescaledScreenWidth  = document.documentElement.clientWidth;
var rescaledScreenHeight = document.documentElement.clientHeight;
```

The next two lines of code in resizeBorder() sets the width and the height properties of the <div> element (whose id attribute has the value outer) equal to the current width and height values, decreased by the quantity 2*borderWidth.

CSS3 MEDIA QUERIES FOR MULTIPLE SCREEN SIZES

In the introduction to CSS3 media queries, you learned about CSS3 media queries and you saw examples of defining media queries with compound conditional logic (which can include and, or, only, and not). In case you didn't already notice, you can use media queries to handle different screen sizes for mobile devices such as smart phones and tablets. An example of doing so is here:

```
@media screen and (min-width: 321px) and (max-width: 480px) {
    div { width: 100px; }
}

@media screen and (min-width: 481px) and (max-width: 720px) {
    div { width: 200px; }
}
```

The logic in the preceding pair of media queries is straightforward: the first media query sets the width of <div> elements to 100px when the screen width is between 321 pixels and 480 pixels; the media query sets the width of <div> elements to 200px when the screen width is between 481 pixels and 720 pixels.

The following media query sets the width of <div> elements to 150px only when it's a screen:

```
@media only screen {
    div { width: 150px; }
}
```

The following media query sets the width of <div> elements to 50px for devices that do not support orientation:

```
not (orientation)  {
    div { width: 50px; }
}
```

As you can see from the examples in this section and in previous sections, CSS3 media queries are simple, flexible, and powerful in terms of their expressiveness and intuitive functionality.

http://docs.webplatform.org/wiki/tutorials/media_queries

CSS FRAMEWORKS AND TOOLKITS

An Appendix on the DVD provides some information about various CSS frameworks (such as `Sass`, `Compass`, and `CSS Scaffold`) that can help you develop code more quickly and also simplify the task of code maintenance. Although you can create CSS stylesheets manually, keep in mind that CSS frameworks provide powerful functionality that is not available in pure CSS3. Two CSS IDEs are Sencha Animator and Adobe Edge Animator, both of which are very powerful IDEs for creating HTML Web pages that contain CSS stylesheets. Perform an Internet search to obtain more information about these and other CSS IDEs.

CSS3 PERFORMANCE

Although this topic is covered briefly here, CSS3 performance is obviously important. Many of the CSS3 stylesheets in this book contain selectors with 2D/3D animation effects, and hardware acceleration will significantly improve performance. In fact, some tablet devices do not provide good hardware acceleration, and stylesheets with many 2D or 3D animation effects are almost impossible on those devices.

Ten items for performance-related CSS3:

http://stackoverflow.com/questions/7486017/css3-what-are-the-performance-best-practices

Fortunately, there is a technique for triggering hardware acceleration for CSS3 selectors (using `translateZ(0)` or `translate3d(0,0,0)`) for devices with a GPU, and also debugging techniques for `Webkit` (Safari and Chrome). The following 30-minute video by Paul Irish (a Developer Advocate at Google) discusses these and other techniques:

http://paulirish.com/2011/dom-html5-css3-performance/

An article that provides information for writing more efficient CSS selectors is here:

http://www.pubnub.com/blog/css3-performance-optimizations

Information regarding "best practices" for writing CSS3 selectors is provided here:

http://webdesignerwall.com/trends/css3-examples-and-best-practices
http://www.impressivewebs.com/css3-best-practices/

Perform an Internet search to find other online videos and tutorials regarding CSS3 performance and "best practices" for CSS3 as well as HTML5 `Canvas`.

SWITCHING TO FULLSCREEN MODE (LIMITED SUPPORT)

Currently, this functionality is only available in Android 4 or higher (on Chrome), partial support in Firefox 12 (or higher) on Android, and also on Meebo. You need to do two things to switch to fullscreen mode. First, verify that the browser supports fullscreen mode, as shown here:

```
if(document.fullScreenEnabled) {
   // do something here
}
```

Second, invoke the `requestFullScreen()` method, as shown here:

```
var elem = document.querySelector("#someIdValue");
var aBtn = document.querySelector("#someButton");

aBtn.addEventListener('click', function () {
   elem.requestFullScreen();
}, false);
```

Keep in mind that this introduces potential security risks, so many devices display a prompt to ensure that users explicitly allow fullscreen mode. The element the method is called on scales up to 100 percent of the device screen's height and width.

Finally, you can enable users to exit fullscreen mode with this code snippet:

```
document.exitFullScreen();
```

CSS3 MEDIA QUERY LISTENERS (IE10 ONLY)

Another new HTML5 feature is media query listeners, and currently there is limited support on mobile devices (but this will change over time). Media query listeners are invoked whenever there is a change in the matching state of a media query expression.

In some cases (such as screen orientation), you can use CSS3 media queries as well as media query listeners to respond to changes of property values.

The following code snippet checks for browser support of media query listeners:

```
if(!!window.matchMedia.addListener) {
    window.matchMedia("(orientation:landscape)")
         .addListener(orientationHandler);
}
```

The following outline shows you how to respond to changes in the orientation of a device (provided that the preceding conditional logic is true):

```
function orientationHandler(mql) {
   if(mql.matches) {
      // do something for landscape
   } else {
      // do something for portrait
   }
}
```

http://docs.webplatform.org/wiki/tutorials/media_queries

USEFUL LINKS

The following alphabetical list of links is short yet useful, and each link contains very good information (and you can always perform your own Internet search as well).

A nice set of "sketch-like" visual effects that use CSS3 is here:

http://andrew-hoyer.com/index.html

Compatibility tables for support of HTML5, CSS3, SVG, and more in desktop and mobile browsers is here:

http://caniuse.com

A Website for generating CSS3 code using various CSS3 features is here:

http://CSS3generator.com

A Website that enables you to perform live editing of the contents of various CSS3 selectors and then see the results is here:

http://CSS3please.com

A toolkit that handles the details of browser-specific extensions for CSS3 properties so that you can write prefix-less CSS3 selectors is here:

http://ecsstender.org

A Website that enables you to create gradients online and view the associated CSS3 code is here:

http://gradients.glrzad.com

Another Website with information regarding browser support for HTML5 and CSS3 features is here:

http://html5readiness.com

An extensive collection of articles regarding HTML5 is available here:

http://www.html5rocks.com/en/

A JavaScript utility that emulates CSS3 pseudo-classes and attribute selectors in IE6-8:

http://selectivizr.com

A Website devoted to all things pertaining to CSS3 is here:

http://www.CSS3.info

An excellent source for browser compatibility information on the Internet (maintained by Peter Paul Koch):

http://www.quirksmode.org

A very good online tool that allows you to experiment with many CSS3 features and also display the associated CSS3 code:

http://www.westciv.com/tools/3Dtransforms/index.html

These links provide a wealth of information and useful techniques, so there's a very good chance that you can find the information that you need to create the visual effects that you want for your Website.

A Website that briefly discusses 14 CSS generators:

http://www.webpop.com/blog/2013/04/23/css-generators

A comparison of 15 cross-browser testing tools (most are free, and some are commercial) with a tabular comparison of features is here:

http://www.smashingmagazine.com/2011/08/07/a-dozen-cross-browser-testing-tools/

SUMMARY

This chapter showed you how to use meta tags in HTML5 Web pages for mobile applications. You saw how to use media queries inline in CSS using `@media` directives in order to conditionally style various HTML elements. You also learned to use CSS3 media queries in order to detect an orientation change of a mobile device, as well as accomplishing the same effect using simple JavaScript code. In addition, you learned how to use CSS3 media queries with conditional logic based on different screen sizes or different screen resolutions, some of which are specific to Android devices and to iOS devices.

HTML5 MOBILE APPS WITH PHONEGAP

This chapter shows you various ways to create HTML5-based hybrid mobile applications for Android and iOS. The code samples in this chapter contain HTML5 and various combinations of HTML5, CSS3, and SVG.

As you will soon discover, this chapter contains more Android-based code samples than iOS-based code samples. The choice of mobile platform for the code samples is purely a stylistic one. However, every Android-based code sample does have an iOS-based counterpart, and vice-versa (both platforms provide the necessary feature support for all the samples in this chapter). Although it was possible to include the same set of code samples for both platforms, doing so would have been needlessly redundant. Moreover, this chapter provides you with the information that you need in order to "convert" an Android-based code sample to its iOS counterpart (and vice versa).

The first part of this chapter provides an overview of how to develop hybrid Android applications using a "manual" approach instead of a toolkit such as PhoneGap. The code samples in this section use the same code that you have seen in earlier chapters, and they show you how to create the hybrid Android mobile applications that will enable you to create the same screenshots. If you feel ambitious, you can create Android-based mobile applications for all the code samples in this book!

The second part of this chapter contains Android-based code samples that show you how to combine native Android applications with CSS3, SVG, and HTML5 Canvas. This section contains an example of rendering a mouse-enabled multi-line graph whose values can be updated whenever users click on the button that is rendered underneath the line graph. Keep in mind that the discussion following the code samples moves quickly because the HTML Web pages contain simple markup, the CSS3 selectors contain code that you have seen in earlier chapters, and the SVG shapes are discussed in an Appendix.

The third part of this chapter provides a quick overview of PhoneGap, which is a popular cross-platform toolkit for developing mobile applications. In 2011, Adobe acquired Nitobi, the company that created PhoneGap, and shortly thereafter Adobe open sourced PhoneGap. This section explains what PhoneGap can do, and also some toolkits that you can use with PhoneGap. You will learn how to create a PhoneGap-based Android application that renders CSS3-based animation effects, and you can deploy this mobile application to Android-based mobile devices that support Android ICS or higher.

The fourth part of this chapter briefly discusses how to create iOS hybrid mobile applications using the PhoneGap plugin for Xcode. The final part of this chapter discusses how to create deploy Android applications to Google Glass.

One point to keep in mind is that the open source project called Apache Cordova comprises a "core" library and a set of files, whereas PhoneGap adds the build tools around Apache Cordova. As you will see in this chapter, PhoneGap allows you to create mobile applications using HTML, CSS, and JavaScript, and you can deploy those mobile applications to numerous platforms, including Android, iOS, BlackBerry, and Windows Mobile. You can also create mobile applications that combine with Sencha Touch (another popular framework), but due to space limitations, Sencha Touch is not discussed in this chapter.

If you are unfamiliar with any of the mobile platforms in this chapter, you can still work through the examples because they consist of HTML5-based code, and the sequence of steps for creating HTML5-based mobile applications on a mobile platform is essentially independent of the actual code.

HTML5/CSS3 AND ANDROID APPLICATIONS

If you are unfamiliar with Android, you can read the Appendix of this book that contains a concise overview of the Android-specific concepts in the code samples in this chapter. You can refer to the appropriate section whenever you encounter an Android concept that is not clear to you.

The code sample in this section shows you how to launch an HTML5 Web page (which also references a CSS3 stylesheet) inside an `Android` application. The key idea consists of three steps:

1) modify the Android `Activity` class to instantiate an Android `Web-View` class, along with some JavaScript-related settings
2) reference an HTML5 Web page that is in the `assets/www` subdirectory of the Android project
3) copy the HTML5 Web page, CSS stylesheets, and JavaScript files into the `assets/www` subdirectory of the Android project

In Step 3 above, you will probably create a hierarchical set of directories that contain files that are of the same type (HTML, CSS, or JavaScript), in much the same way that you organize your files in a Web application.

Now launch Eclipse and create an Android project called `AndroidCSS3`, making sure that you select Android version 3.1 or higher, which is necessary in order to render CSS3-based effects.

After you have created the project, let's take a look at four files that contain the custom code for this Android mobile application. Listings 5.1, 5.2, and 5.3 display the contents of `main.xml`, `AndroidCSS3.html`, and `AndroidC-SS3Activity.java`.

LISTING 5.1: *main.xml*

```
<?xml version="1.0" encoding="utf-8"?>
<LinearLayout xmlns:android="http://schemas.android.com/apk/res/android"
    android:orientation="vertical"
    android:layout_width="fill_parent"
    android:layout_height="fill_parent">
  <WebView android:id="@+id/webview"
          android:layout_width="fill_parent"
          android:layout_height="fill_parent">
  </WebView>
</LinearLayout>
```

Listing 5.1 specifies a `LinearLayout` that contains an Android `Web-View` that will occupy the entire screen of the mobile device. This is the behavior that we want to see, because Android default browser is rendered inside the Android `WebView`.

LISTING 5.2: *AndroidCSS3.html*

```
<!doctype html>
<head>
  <title>CSS Radial Gradient Example</title>
  <link href="AndroidCSS3.css" rel="stylesheet">
</head>

<body>
 <div id="outer">
  <div id="radial1">Text1</div>
  <div id="radial2">Text2</div>
  <div id="radial3">Text3</div>
  <div id="radial4">Text4</div>
 </div>
</body>
</html>
```

Listing 5.2 is a straightforward HTML Web page that references a CSS stylesheet `AndroidCSS3.css` (that is available on the DVD), along with an HTML `<div>` element (whose `id` attribute has value `outer`) that serves as a "container" for four more HTML `<div>` elements.

The CSS stylesheet `AndroidCSS3.css` contains a CSS selector for styling the HTML `<div>` element whose `id` has value `outer`, followed by four CSS selectors `radial1`, `radial2`, `radial3`, and `radial4` that are used to style the corresponding HTML <div> elements in Listing 5.2. The contents of these selectors ought to be very familiar (you can review the material for CSS3 gradients in an earlier chapter), so we will not cover their contents in this section.

LISTING 5.3: AndroidCSS3Activity.java

```
package com.iquarkt.css3;

import android.app.Activity;
import android.os.Bundle;

import android.webkit.WebChromeClient;
import android.webkit.WebSettings;
import android.webkit.WebView;
import android.webkit.WebViewClient;

public class AndroidCSS3Activity extends Activity
{
    /** Called when the activity is first created. */
    @Override
    public void onCreate(Bundle savedInstanceState)
    {
        super.onCreate(savedInstanceState);
        setContentView(R.layout.main);

        // Get a reference to the declared WebView holder
        WebView webview = (WebView) this.findViewById(R.id.webview);

        // Get the settings
        WebSettings webSettings = webview.getSettings();

        // Enable Javascript for interaction
        webSettings.setJavaScriptEnabled(true);

        // Make the zoom controls visible
        webSettings.setBuiltInZoomControls(true);

        // Allow for touching selecting/deselecting data series
        webview.requestFocusFromTouch();

        // Load the URL
        webview.loadUrl("file:///android_asset/AndroidCSS3.html");
    }
}
```

Listing 5.3 defines a Java class AndroidCSS3Activity that extends the standard Android Activity class. This class contains the onCreate() method that "points" to the XML document main.xml (displayed in Listing 5.2) so that we can get a reference to its WebView child element via R.id.webview (which is the reference to the WebView element in Listing 5.2), as shown here:

```
WebView webview = (WebView) this.findViewById(R.id.webview);
```

Next, the `webSettings` instance of the `WebSettings` class enables us to set various properties, as shown in the commented lines of code in Listing 5.3.

The final line of code loads the contents of the HTML Web page `AndroidCSS3.html` (which is in the `assets/www` subdirectory), as shown here:

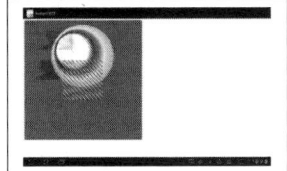

FIGURE 5.1 A CSS3-based 3D Cube on an Asus Prime Tablet with Android ICS.

```
webview.loadUrl("file:///android_asset/AndroidCSS3.html");
```

Figure 5.1 displays a CSS3-based `Android` application on an Asus Prime tablet with `Android` ICS.

SVG AND ANDROID APPLICATIONS

The example in this section shows you how to create an Android mobile application that renders SVG code that is embedded in an HTML5 Web page. Now launch Eclipse and create an Android project called `AndroidSVG1`, making sure that you select Android version 3.1 or higher, which is necessary in order to render SVG elements.

The example in the previous section contains four custom files, whereas the Android/SVG example in this section contains two files with custom code: the HTML5 Web page `AndroidSVG1.html` in Listing 5.4 and the Java class `AndroidSVG1.java`, which available on the DVD.

LISTING 5.4: AndroidSVG1.html

```
<!DOCTYPE html>
<html>
  <body>
    <h1>HTML5/SVG Example</h1>
    <svg>
      <ellipse cx="300" cy="50" rx="80" ry="40"
               fill="#ff0" stroke-dasharray="8 4 8 1"
               style="stroke:red;stroke-width:4;"/>

      <line x1="100" y1="20" x2="300" y2="350"
               stroke-dasharray="8 4 8 1"
               style="stroke:red;stroke-width:8;"/>

      <g transform="translate(20,20)">
        <path
          d="M0,0 C200,150 400,300 20,250"
          fill="#f00"
          stroke-dasharray="4 4 4 4"
          style="stroke:blue;stroke-width:4;"/>
      </g>
```

```
    <g transform="translate(200,50)">
      <path
        d="M200,150 C0,0 400,300 20,250"
        fill="#00f"
        stroke-dasharray="12 12 12 12"
        style="stroke:blue;stroke-width:4;"/>
    </g>
  </svg>
 </body>
</html>
```

Listing 5.4 is an HTML Web page that contains an SVG document with the definitions for an ellipse, a line segment, and two cubic Bezier curves. Appendix A contains examples of these 2D shapes (among others), and you can review the appropriate material if you need to refresh your memory.

The Java class `AndroidSVG1Activity.java` is omitted, but its contents are very similar to Listing 5.3, and the complete source code is available on the DVD.

Figure 5.2 displays an SVG -based `Android` application on an Asus Prime tablet with `Android` ICS.

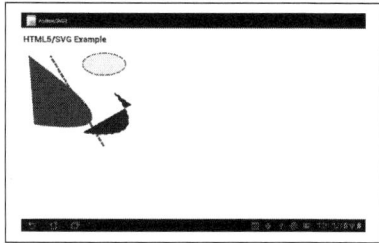

FIGURE 5.2 An SVG-based Android application on an Asus Tablet with Android ICS.

HTML5 CANVAS AND ANDROID APPLICATIONS

In addition to rendering CSS3-based effects and SVG documents, you can also render `Canvas`-based 2D shapes in an Android application. Launch Eclipse and create an Android project called `AndroidCanvas1`, making sure that you select Android version 3.1 or higher, which is necessary in order to render SVG elements.

The example in this section contains one custom file called `AndroidCanvas1.html`, which is displayed in Listing 5.5.

LISTING 5.5: AndroidCanvas1.html

```
<!DOCTYPE html>
<html lang="en">
<head>
 <meta charset="utf-8" />
 <title>HTML5 Canvas Example</title>

<script>
 function draw() {
   var basePointX  = 10;
   var basePointY  = 80;
   var currentX    = 0;
   var currentY    = 0;
```

```
var startAngle  = 0;
var endAngle    = 0;
var radius      = 120;
var lineLength  = 200;
var lineWidth   = 1;
var lineCount   = 200;
var lineColor   = "";

var hexArray    = new Array('0','1','2','3','4','5','6','7',
                            '8','9','a','b','c','d','e','f');

var can = document.getElementById('canvas1');
var ctx = can.getContext('2d');

// render a text string...
ctx.font = "bold 26px helvetica, arial, sans-serif";
ctx.shadowColor = "#333333";
ctx.shadowOffsetX = 2;
ctx.shadowOffsetY = 2;
ctx.shadowBlur = 2;
ctx.fillStyle = 'red';
ctx.fillText("HTML5 Canvas/Android", 0, 30);

for(var r=0; r<lineCount; r++) {
    currentX = basePointX+r;
    currentY = basePointY+r;
    startAngle = (360-r/2)*Math.PI/180;
    endAngle   = (360+r/2)*Math.PI/180;

    // render the first line segment...
    lineColor = '#' + hexArray[r%16] + '00';
    ctx.strokeStyle = lineColor;
    ctx.lineWidth   = lineWidth;

    ctx.beginPath();
    ctx.moveTo(currentX, currentY+2*r);
    ctx.lineTo(currentX+lineLength, currentY+2*r);
    ctx.closePath();
    ctx.stroke();
    ctx.fill();

    // render the second line segment...
    lineColor = '#' + '0' + hexArray[r%16] + '0';
    ctx.beginPath();
    ctx.moveTo(currentX, currentY);
    ctx.lineTo(currentX+lineLength, currentY);
    ctx.closePath();
    ctx.stroke();
    ctx.fill();

    // render the arc...
    lineColor = '#' + '00'+ hexArray[(2*r)%16];
    ctx.beginPath();
    ctx.fillStyle = lineColor;
    ctx.moveTo(currentX, currentY);
```

```
            ctx.arc(currentX, currentY, radius,
                    startAngle, endAngle, false);
            ctx.closePath();
            ctx.stroke();
            ctx.fill();
        }
    }
}
</script>
</head>

<body onload="draw()">
    <canvas id="canvas1" width="300px" height="200px"></canvas>
</body>
<html>
```

Listing 5.5 contains some boilerplate HTML markup and a JavaScript function `draw()` that is executed when the Web page is loaded into the Android browser. The `draw()` function contains JavaScript code that draws a set of line segments and arcs into the HTML5 `<canvas>` element whose `id` attribute has value `canvas1`. You can read online tutorials that have similar functionality if you don't remember the details of the syntax of this JavaScript code.

Figure 5.3 displays a `Canvas`-based `Android` application on an Asus Prime tablet with `Android` ICS.

The next portion of this chapter delves into PhoneGap, which is a toolkit that automatically creates the lower level "scaffolding" that you performed manually in the previous part of this chapter. You will get instructions for installing the PhoneGap plugin for Eclipse to create Android mobile applications, and later in this chapter you will also learn how to install the PhoneGap plugin for Xcode in order to create HTML5-based mobile applications for iOS mobile devices.

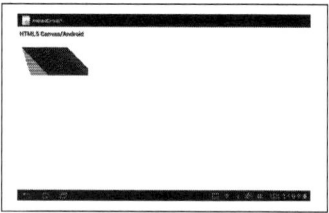

FIGURE 5.3 A Canvas-based Android application on an Asus Tablet with Android ICS.

WHAT IS PHONEGAP?

PhoneGap is an open source device agnostic mobile application development tool that enables you to create cross-platform mobile applications using CSS, HTML, and JavaScript, and its homepage is here:

http://phonegap.com

The PhoneGap homepage provides documentation, code samples, and a download link for the PhoneGap distribution.

PhoneGap enables you to create HTML-based mobile application for Android, Blackberry, iPhone, Palm, Symbian, and Windows Mobile. PhoneGap provides support for touch events, event listeners, rendering images, database access, different file formats (XML and JSON), and Web Services.

Note that if you want to develop iPhone applications, you must have a Macbook or some other OS X machine, along with other dependencies that are discussed later in this chapter.

How Does PhoneGap Work?

PhoneGap mobile applications involve a Web view that is embedded in a native "shell," and your custom code runs in the Web view. In addition, Phone-Gap provides a JavaScript API for accessing native features of a mobile device, and your code can use PhoneGap in order to access those native features. For example, PhoneGap contains JavaScript APIs for accessing Accelerometer, Camera, Compass, Contacts, Device information, Events, Geolocation, Media, Notification, and Storage.

Keep in mind that PhoneGap does not provide HTML UI elements, so if you need this functionality in your mobile applications, you can add other toolkits and frameworks, such as jQuery Mobile, Sencha Touch, or Appcelerator.

Software Dependencies for PhoneGap 3.0

In order to install PhoneGap 3.0, you must first install NodeJS on your machine. NodeJS is required if you want to install any plugins (including the core plugins) into your application. The development team chose NodeJS in order to build tools that work in a cross-platform fashion, using a single code base.

The examples in this chapter show you how to create hybrid applications using PhoneGap 3.0, which has simplified the process for creating mobile applications compared to earlier versions of PhoneGap. However, if you do not want to install NodeJS, PhoneGap 2.9 (as well as the earlier releases in the 2.x series) is a downloadable distribution that you can install in Eclipse or Xcode.

Note: This chapter does not provide many details about PhoneGap version 2.9 because version 3.0 is the recommended version.

CREATING ANDROID HYBRID APPLICATIONS WITH PHONEGAP 3.0

The first step is to install NodeJS on your machine, and you can download a pre-built installer for your platform here:

http://nodejs.org/download/

Now install PhoneGap with the following command on Mac laptops:

```
sudo npm install -g phonegap
```

You can check the version of PhoneGap with the following command:

```
phonegap -v
```

You will see something like the following (the version number might be different when you perform the installation):

```
3.0.0-0.14.3
```

Now create an PhoneGap 3.0 project by executing the following three commands:

```
phonegap create my-app
cd my-app
phonegap run android
```

After you invoke the third command listed above, you will see something like this on the command line:

```
[phonegap] detecting Android SDK environment...
[phonegap] using the local environment
[phonegap] adding the Android platform...
[warning] missing library cordova/android/3.0.0
[phonegap] downloading https://git-wip-
us.apache.org/repos/asf?p=cordova-
android.git;a=snapshot;h=3.0.0;sf=tgz...
[phonegap] compiling Android...
[phonegap] successfully compiled Android app
[phonegap] trying to install app onto device
[phonegap] no device was found
[phonegap] trying to install app onto emulator
```

If you have an Android mobile device attached to your machine, you will not see the last pair of lines in the preceding output; instead, you will see the HTML5 Web page index.html rendered on the screen of the Android mobile device that you have attached to your machine via the USB port.

One point to keep in mind is that PhoneGap generates 300 files in the my-app directory, and this generic "Hello World" application consists of slightly more than 7 megabytes. Some of the main files of interest in this mobile application are here:

```
./platforms/android/AndroidManifest.xml
./platforms/android/assets/www/index.html
./platforms/android/assets/www/phonegap.js
./platforms/android/bin/HelloWorld-debug.apk
./platforms/android/src/com/phonegap/hello_world/HelloWorld.java
```

The HTML Web page index.html (listed in bold in the preceding list) is the Web page that is launched inside a WebView component in the generated Android apk when it is launched in a Simulator or an Android device.

Listing 5.6 displays the contents of HelloWorld.java.

LISTING 5.6: HelloWorld.java

```
/*
          Licensed to the Apache Software Foundation (ASF) under one
          or more contributor license agreements. See the NOTICE file
          distributed with this work for additional information
          regarding copyright ownership. The ASF licenses this file
          to you under the Apache License, Version 2.0 (the
          "License"); you may not use this file except in compliance
          with the License. You may obtain a copy of the License at
```

```
       http://www.apache.org/licenses/LICENSE-2.0

    Unless required by applicable law or agreed to in writing,
    software distributed under the License is distributed on an
    "AS IS" BASIS, WITHOUT WARRANTIES OR CONDITIONS OF ANY
    KIND, either express or implied. See the License for the
    specific language governing permissions and limitations
    under the License.
 */

package com.phonegap.hello_world;

import android.os.Bundle;
import org.apache.cordova.*;

public class HelloWorld extends DroidGap
{
    @Override
    public void onCreate(Bundle savedInstanceState)
    {
        super.onCreate(savedInstanceState);

        // Set by <content src="index.html" /> in config.xml
        super.loadUrl(Config.getStartUrl());
        //super.loadUrl("file:///android_asset/www/index.html")
    }
}
```

Listing 5.6 contains `import` statements that reference a standard Android class and the classes in the package `org.apache.cordova`. The next portion of code defines the Android class `HelloWorld` that extends the `DroidGap` class. Next, the method `onCreate()` invokes the `onCreate()` method of the super class, and then references the HTML Web page `index.html` that is in the following subdirectory of `my-app` (the top-level directory for this project):

```
./platforms/android/assets/www/index.html
```

This concludes the brief introduction to generating hybrid mobile applications using version 3.0 of PhoneGap, and you can find additional information about PhoneGap 3.0 here:

http://docs.phonegap.com/en/3.0.0/index.html

The following variation of the preceding steps shows you can also specify the package name when you create a PhoneGap Android hybrid mobile application for Android from the command line:

```
cordova create HelloWorld com.example.hello "HelloWorld"
cd HelloWorld
cordova platform add android
cordova build
cordova run android
```

If you want to launch the preceding application in the Android simulator, use the following command:

```
cordova emulate android
```

Note: Make sure that you do not use spaces when you specify "HelloWorld."

CREATING IOS HYBRID APPLICATIONS WITH PHONEGAP 3.0

Follow the steps in the preceding section for installing NodeJS and Phone-Gap 3.0 on your machine. Next create the my-app project (also discussed in the preceding section) and add an iOS application with the following command:

```
cordova platform add ios
cordova build
cordova run ios
```

If you see the following error message:

```
[Error: Xcode version installed is too old. Minimum: >=4.5.x, yours:
Error:]
```

You need to invoke the following command (adjust the subdirectory of / Applications to match the one on your machine):

```
sudo xcode-select --switch /Applications/Xcode5-
DP2.app/Contents/Developer
```

This concludes the introduction to PhoneGap, and the next portion of this chapter provides an overview of Google Glass, which is an interesting (and perhaps even controversial) Google device.

WORKING WITH HTML5, PHONEGAP, AND IOS

This section shows you how to create iOS mobile applications using Phone-Gap, which is exactly the process that was used to create the iOS mobile applications in this book, whose screenshots on an iPad3 are included in various chapters. Every iOS mobile application in this book was developed on a Macbook OS X 10.8.2 with Apple's Xcode 4.5 and PhoneGap.

Earlier in this chapter you learned how to create Android applications in Eclipse, which is an IDE that runs on multiple OSes, but the situation is different for creating iOS applications (with or without PhoneGap).

First, you need access to an Apple device (such as a Macbook, Mac Mini, or Mac Pro) with Apple's Xcode installed in order to create mobile applications for iOS mobile devices. If you register as a developer you can download for free, or for $4.99 in the Apple iStore. Although this section uses Xcode 4.5, it's possible to install a lower version of Xcode (but make sure that you check the minimum required version for OS X).

Second, you need to install the PhoneGap plugin for Xcode, as described earlier in this chapter.

Third, you need to register as an Apple Developer (which costs $99 USD per year *if you want to deploy your iOS mobile applications to iOS devices*). However, if you only plan to use the iOS Simulator, you can do so at no charge.

After you have set up a laptop with the required software, you will be ready to create an iOS mobile application with PhoneGap, which is the topic of the next section.

Note: PhoneGap applications always have the same filename `index.html`, so in order to provide multiple PhoneGap project files in the same directory on the DVD, the HTML Web page `index.html` for each PhoneGap project is saved in a Web page whose name is the same as the project.

A CSS3 CUBE ON IOS USING PHONEGAP

For the final code sample in this chapter, create an Xcode application called `ThreeDCube1` by selecting the PhoneGap plugin (make sure that your filenames start with an alphabetic character or you will get errors when you attempt to compile and deploy your applications). Copy the CSS stylesheet `ThreeD-Cube1.css` into your project, and replace `index.html` with the HTML Web page `ThreeDCube1.html` in your project.

Note that if you are using Xcode 4.x with a PhoneGap plugin from an earlier version of PhoneGap, then you need to perform a manual copy of the generated www subdirectory into the project home directory of your current Xcode application. When you have performed this step correctly, you will no longer see an error message when you launch your mobile application in the Simulator or on your iOS device.

Listing 5.7 displays the contents of the HTML Web page `ThreeDCube1.html` that references a CSS stylesheet that creates animation effects.

LISTING 5.7: ThreeDCube1.html

```
<!DOCTYPE html>
<!--
    Licensed to the Apache Software Foundation (ASF) under one
    or more contributor license agreements.  See the NOTICE file
    distributed with this work for additional information
    regarding copyright ownership.  The ASF licenses this file
    to you under the Apache License, Version 2.0 (the
    "License"); you may not use this file except in compliance
    with the License.  You may obtain a copy of the License at

    http://www.apache.org/licenses/LICENSE-2.0

    Unless required by applicable law or agreed to in writing,
    software distributed under the License is distributed on an
    "AS IS" BASIS, WITHOUT WARRANTIES OR CONDITIONS OF ANY
     KIND, either express or implied.  See the License for the
    specific language governing permissions and limitations
    under the License.
-->
```

```
<html>
    <head>
        <meta charset="utf-8" />
        <meta name="format-detection" content="telephone=no" />
        <meta name="viewport" content="user-scalable=no, initial-
scale=1, maximum-scale=1, minimum-scale=1, width=device-width,
height=device-height, target-densitydpi=device-dpi" />

<!-- commented out to prevent logo.png from being displayed:
        <link rel="stylesheet" type="text/css" href="css/index.
css" />
-->
        <link href="ThreeDCube1.css" rel="stylesheet" type="text/
css">
        <title>CSS 3D Cube Example</title>
    </head>

    <body>
      <div id="outer">
       <div id="top">Text1</div>
       <div id="left">Text2</div>
       <div id="right">Text3</div>
      </div>

      <div class="app">
<!-- commented out to remove default PhoneGap text messages:
        <h1>PhoneGap</h1>
        <div id="deviceready" class="blink">
            <p class="event listening">Connecting to Device</p>
            <p class="event received">Device is Ready</p>
        </div>
-->
      </div>

      <script type="text/javascript" src="phonegap.js"></script>
      <script type="text/javascript" src="js/index.js"></script>
      <script type="text/javascript">
          app.initialize();
      </script>
    </body>
</html>
```

Listing 5.7 is the result of merging the HTML Web page ThreeDCube1. html with the HTML Web page index.html that is automatically generated by PhoneGap. The first part of Listing 5.7 contains a copyright notice, followed by boilerplate HTML markup, and then a <link> element that references the CSS stylesheet ThreeDCube1.css (shown in Listing 5.8). The next portion of code contains a <body> element, followed by some markup that originates from the Web page ThreeDCube1.html. The remaining portion of Listing 5.7 contains auto-generated code that references the appropriate JavaScript files to perform PhoneGap-related initialization.

Listing 5.8 displays a portion of the contents of the CSS stylesheet Three-DCube1.css that contains CSS selectors for creating animation effects. The entire contents of ThreeDCube1.css are available on the DVD.

LISTING 5.8: ThreeDCube1.css

```
@-webkit-keyframes animCube1 {
    0% {
        -webkit-transform: matrix(1.5, 0.5,  0.0, 1.5, 0, 0)
                           matrix(1.0, 0.0,  1.0, 1.0, 0, 0);
    }

    10% {
        -webkit-transform: translate3d(50px,50px,50px)
rotate3d(50px,50px,50px,-90deg) skew(-15deg,0) scale3d(1.25, 1.25,
1.25);
    }
    // details omitted for brevity
}

#outer {
-webkit-animation-name: animCube1;
-webkit-animation-duration: 40s;
}
// more details omitted for brevity
```

Notice that Listing 5.8 defines a CSS3 `keyframes` rule called `animCube1` that is referenced in the selector `#outer`, which in turn matches an HTML `<div>` element in Listing 5.7 that "encloses" the 3D cube.

Now run this mobile application, either in the Xcode Simulator or on your mobile device, and you will see a graphics image that is similar to Figure 5.4.

The process for creating the other iOS-based mobile applications in this chapter is identical to the process for the preceding iOS mobile application, so there is no need to include additional examples. However, it's worth your while to spend some time creating additional iOS mobile applications, which will increase your comfort level, and perhaps also motivate you to learn about other features of Xcode.

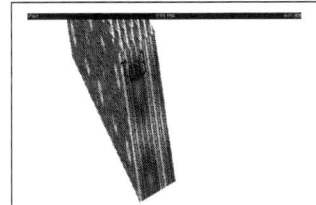

FIGURE 5.4 A CSS3 Cube on an iPad3.

FIREFOX OS FOR HYBRID MOBILE APPS

Although the focus of this chapter is PhoneGap, Firefox OS is an emerging mobile application development environment.

You can use Firefox OS to create packaged mobile applications and hosted applications.

A packaged application involves creating a zip file that contains all the assets (such as HTML, CSS, JavaScript, images, and so forth) of an application. You distribute the packaged application via that zip file. By contrast, the assets of a hosted application are maintained on the server, which means that its functionality is similar to that of a Website.

Both types of applications require a valid manifest file, and you can list both of them in the Firefox Marketplace. You distribute packaged applications by uploading a zip file to the marketplace. For hosted applications, you provide a URL and the Firefox Marketplace links to the install location.

A manifest file is a JSON file that identifies the application and the values of some variables. Listing 5.9 displays the contents of a sample manifest file.

LISTING 5.9: A Firefox OS Manifest file

```
{
  "name": "My App",
  "description": "My elevator pitch goes here",
  "launch_path": "/",
  "icons": {
    "128": "/img/icon-128.png"
  },
  "developer": {
    "name": "Your name or organization",
    "url": "http://your-homepage-here.org"
  },
  "default_locale": "en"
}
```

A manifest file can contain many other entries, including activities, appcache_path, csp, default_locale, description, developer, fullscreen, icons, installs_allowed_from, and various others. More detailed information and examples are available here:

https://developer.mozilla.org/en-US/docs/Web/Apps/Manifest

At its core, Firefox OS mobile applications use JavaScript APIs, and the associated manifest file specifies restricted APIs (if any). During the application installation phase, users can approve the requested permissions (which users can change later), in much the same way that Facebook applications request access permissions.

The significant advantage of Firefox OS applications is the freedom of the Web to create the functionality that you need without being restricted by the approval process. In addition, there is an approval process for submitting applications to the Mozilla Marketplace that is much simpler than Google Play or Apple's App Store.

Keep in mind that Firefox OS is an ambitious yet still unproven platform. Mozilla calls Firefox OS "the platform HTML5 deserves," and the extent to which this is true remains to be seen.

OTHER TOOLKITS AND FRAMEWORKS FOR HYBRID MOBILE APPS

In addition to PhoneGap and Firefox OS, there are other toolkits and frameworks available for developing hybrid HTML5 mobile applications. These alternatives also have different strengths and weaknesses, and some of them have free as well as commercial options.

One popular framework is Appcelerator Titanium, and its homepage is here:

http://www.appcelerator.com/

Appcelerator Titanium provides an end-to-end development environment for developing iOS and Android mobile applications. Appcelerator Titanium is an open source framework for building native applications. You have access to most features in mobile devices, with future support for running applications in the background.

Another alternative is Sencha Touch, which is a framework for mobile application development that supports WebKit (and also added support for IE in 2013). The Sencha homepage is here:

http://www.sencha.com/

You can use Sencha Touch in conjunction with PhoneGap, whereas Appcelerator has its own UI components. Sencha Touch is open source, but you must buy a license if you use it for commercial purposes. Sencha Touch works inside the browser of mobile devices, and you can use it with PhoneGap to access device features. The Sencha Touch framework is loaded first, followed by the application content, so there will be a slight performance penalty during application start-up. In addition, Sencha touch runs in various simulators, including iPhone, Android, and Blackberry.

Two other products are Sencha Animator (a free IDE that supports HTML5 and CSS3) and Sencha Architect, which is a commercial product.

These toolkits and frameworks have other features that are not discussed in this section, so it's important to evaluate them using various criteria, such as:

- feature support
- ease of development
- performance
- the learning curve for the toolkit
- your technical requirements
- your budget

In case you want to focus entirely on mobile devices, there are also mobile-only toolkits available, such as LungoJS (*http://lungo.tapquo.com*) and Jo (*http://joapp.com*), both of which support multiple mobile devices.

HYBRID HTML5 MOBILE APPLICATIONS FOR GOOGLE GLASS

Google Glass is a portable "hands free" wearable device that supports Android 4.0.3 (Ice Cream Sandwich). Google Glass enables you to issue voice commands to take pictures (simply say "take a picture"), get directions, ask for information ("how long is the Brooklyn bridge"), and even translate your voice into a different language ("say half a pound in Chinese"). As you can imagine, the ability to issue voice commands enables you to capture spontaneous events that might otherwise be lost because they only lasted for a few seconds and you didn't have a camera or enough time to take a picture or video.

When tethered to your phone, Google Glass can also make calls and send text messages. You can also use Google Glass with an Android phone in order to screen-cast what is currently display in Google Glass.

As this book goes to print, Google Glass will use OLED displays from Samsung. OLED is transparent, flexible, and almost unbreakable, which will make Google Glass a very durable product.

As a developer, you can interact with a user's timeline by invoking the appropriate RESTful endpoint to perform the desired action. Google handles the necessary details of synchronizing between your Glassware and your users' Glass.

Some common actions that you can perform include:

• Creating and managing timeline cards on a user's Glass
• Subscribing to notifications from Glass to be notified of user actions
• Obtaining a user's location

How Does Google Glass Work?

Google Glass provides software called Glassware that enables you to develop Glass mobile applications. Google Glass supports the Google Mirror API, which is a set of RESTful services that transmit information to and receive notifications from Glass devices. The Google Mirror API Playground is available for experimenting with how content is displayed on Glass:

https://developers.google.com/glass/playground

Google Glass uses a timeline that contains so-called "cards," each of which is used to display information to users. Users navigate through their own timeline by swiping backward and forward on Glass, thereby displaying cards in the past and future.

Each timeline card contains information pushed to Glass devices from various pieces of Glassware. In addition, there are default timeline cards that are "pinned" to a timeline, so they always appear in the same place. The card that displays the current time and the card that displays all of the tasks that Glass can execute are examples of pinned cards.

Many timeline cards have additional interactions associated with them that are accessible with a single tap. You can define these menu items to allow users to execute actions such as deleting or sharing a card.

Currently, Google Glass provides a browser, which means that you can deploy and render HTML5 Web pages containing JavaScript, SVG, or HTML5 `<canvas>` elements to Google Glass if they are rendered in a `WebView` component. Consequently, you can deploy the hybrid HTML5 Web applications in this book to Google Glass. The details of deploying to Google Glass (which involves the Android `adb` utility) are discussed later in this chapter.

Before discussing the deployment of Android mobile applications to Google Glass, let's take a quick look at the set of HTML5 tags that are support (and also not supported) in Google Glass applications, which are listed in the next two sections.

Supported HTML5 Tags

There are various allowed HTML elements when using the Glass Mirror API. The allowed HTML elements are elements that you can use in timeline cards. Allowed header tags are h1, h2, h3, h4, h5, and h6. Allowed image tags are img. Allowed list tags are li, ol, and ul. Allowed HTML5 semantic tags are article, aside, details, figure, figcaption, footer, header, nav, section, summary, and time. Allowed structural tags are blockquote, br, div, hr, p, and span. Allowed style tags are b, big, center, em, i, u, s, small, strike, strong, style, sub, and sup. Allowed table-related tags are table, tbody, td, tfoot, th, thead, and tr.

Unsupported HTML5 Tags

Blocked HTML elements (and their contents) are removed from HTML payloads. Blocked Document headers are head, title Embeds: audio, embed, object, source, and video. Blocked Frames tags are frame and frameset. Blocked scripting tags are applet and script. Any elements not listed above are removed, but their contents are preserved.

Deploying Android Apps to Google Glass

The good news is that none of the preceding restrictions for HTML elements are applicable when you launch a `WebView` in a native Android application. You can deploy Android applications to Google Glass using the `adb` command from the command line, in the same way that you can deploy Android applications to other Android mobile devices via the command line.

For example, you can deploy the Android application `ThreeDCube1.apk` (available on the DVD) to Google Glass by performing the following steps:

1. connect a USB cable from your machine to Google Glass
2. navigate to the directory with the Android apk file
3. run the command: `adb install ThreeDCube1.apk`

After completing the preceding steps, you launch the Android apk file via the `adb` utility from the command line by specifying the fully qualified package name of the Android activity and the name of the `Activity`. In the case of the Android Web application `ThreeDCube1`, the package name is `com.iquarkt.graphics` and the name of the Android `Activity` is `ThreeD-Cube1Activity`, so the command looks like this:

```
adb shell am start -a android.intent.action.MAIN -n
com.iquarkt.css3/.ThreeDCube1Activity
```

After issuing the preceding command, tap the Google Glass and after a few moments you ought to see the "flying 3D cube" appear in Google Glass.

Displaying Google Glass in an Emulator

You can also display whatever is being rendered in Google Glass in an emulator that you can launch from the command line. You need to launch the JAR file whose name starts with `asm` (followed by an Android version number) that is located in the directory `$ANDROID_TOP/tools/lib`. For example, the command that you need to invoke for Android 4.0.x is shown here:

```
java -jar $ANDROID_TOP/tools/lib/asm-4.0.jar
```

Now select one of the hybrid HTML5 mobile applications for Android in this chapter, deploy it to Google Glass, and then launch the preceding command so that you can view that Android application running in the Emulator while it's simultaneously running on Google Glass.

One point to keep in mind is that there is a time delay on the emulator, and the transitions are not quite as smooth as they are in Google Glass.

Figure 5.5 displays a screenshot of the Android mobile application `ThreeDCube1.apk` that was deployed to Google Glass, launched from the command line, and a screenshot was then taken in the Emulator. Note that the image has a grainy appearance in the Emulator, but its resolution is better in Google Glass.

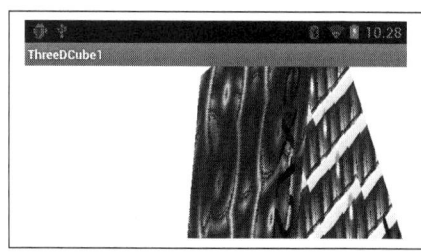

FIGURE 5.5 A CSS3 3D Cube Rendered in Google Glass.

Other Useful Links for Google Glass

The PlayGround site to test how an HTML card is rendered:

https://developers.google.com/glass/playground

If you want to see a fully deployed version of the starter project to get an idea of how it works before you start your own development, navigate to this link:

https://glass-java-starter-demo.appspot.com/

If you are planning to develop Google Glass applications, make sure that you read the developer policies here:

https://developers.google.com/glass/policies

Various Google Glass "starter projects" (available in Java, Python, and PHP) are here:

https://developers.google.com/glass/downloads/

Other Google Glass Code Samples

Lance Nanek has created some interesting Google Glass applications that you can view on github:

https://github.com/lnanek

This concludes our coverage of Google Glass in this chapter. Although Google Glass is still in its infancy, it has tremendous potential in terms of the set of applications that developers can create for this mobile device.

ADDITIONAL CODE SAMPLES ON THE DVD

Although Android does not have built-in support for rendering charts and graphs, you can create them using `Canvas`-based code that is very similar to the code in the previous section.

Launch Eclipse and create an Android project called `AndroidCanvasMultiLine2`, making sure that you select Android version 3.1 or higher. The HTML5 Web page `AndroidCanvasMultiLine2.html` on the DVD contains JavaScript code for rendering multiple line graphs using HTML5 `Canvas`.

Figure 5.5 displays a `Canvas`-based multi-line graph `Android` application on a Nexus S 4G with Android ICS.

The Android project `HTML5CanvasBBall2` contains the HTML5 Web page `HTML5CanvasBBall2.html` that contains JavaScript code for creating a bouncing ball effect in HTML5 `Canvas`.

The Android project `PhoneGapForm1` contains the HTML5 Web page `PhoneGapForm1.html` (which will actually be named `index.html` in your Android project) that illustrates how to create a form for various types of user input in PhoneGap, and the types of the input fields are such that the following occurs when users navigate to this form:

FIGURE 5.5 A Canvas-based Multi-Line Graph on an Android Smart Phone.

- text input displays a standard keyboard
- telephone input displays a telephone keypad
- URL input displays a URL keyboard
- E-mail input displays an email keyboard
- zipcode input displays a numeric keyboard

SUMMARY

This chapter showed you how to create hybrid Android mobile applications that contain HTML5, CSS3, and SVG. You created such mobile applications manually, which involved creating Android projects in Eclipse, and then modifying the contents of the Android Activity class and populating an assets subdirectory with HTML-related files.

Next, you learned how to use the PhoneGap Eclipse plugin, which simplifies the process of creating an Android project. You also saw how the PhoneGap plugin creates a default page that allows you to use "live" features of your Android device.

HTML5 MEDIA AND DEVICE ACCESS

This chapter starts with a discussion of the new HTML5 `<audio>` and `<video>` elements for playing audio and video clips. Next, you'll learn about the Web Audio APIs, along with a code sample that illustrates how to convert an audio file into a graphical representation using the HTML5 `<canvas>` element. The final portion of this chapter delves into some hardware-related APIs, including accelerometer and battery, with code samples that illustrate how to use them.

THE HTML5 `<AUDIO>` ELEMENT

The HTML5 `<audio>` tag is very simple to use, and its syntax looks like this:

```
<audio src="Sample1.mp3" controls autoplay loop>
  HTML5 audio tag not supported
</audio>
```

The HTML5 `<audio>` tag supports several attributes, including `auto-play` (play the audio as soon as it's ready), `controls` (displays the `play`, `pause`, and `volume` controls), `loop` (replays the audio), `preload` (loads the audio so it's ready to run on page load), and `src` (specifies the location of the audio file).

Note: In iOS the `autoplay` attribute does nothing until users tap the screen.

A minimalistic example of how to use the `<audio>` tag in an HTML5 Web page is illustrated in Listing 6.1, which displays the contents of `HTML5Au-dio1.html`.

LISTING 6.1 HTML5Audio1.html

```
<!doctype html>
<html>
<head>
  <meta charset="utf-8" />
  <title>HTML5 Audio</title>
</head>

<body>
  <h1>Audio Recording in Japanese</h1>

  <!-- Display control buttons -->
  <audio src="Japanese1.m4a" controls autoplay loop>
    HTML5 audio tag not supported  </audio>
 </body>
</html>
```

Listing 6.1 is very straightforward: boilerplate code and one HTML5
<audio> element that specifies the audio file Japanese1.m4a, along with
audio controls that enable users to replay the audio clip.

Different browsers support different audio file formats; fortunately, the
HTML5 <audio> tag supports a <source> element, which in turn provides
an src attribute that enables you to specify different file formats, as shown here:

```
<audio controls="true">
   <source src="s.mp3" type="audio/mp3">
   <source src="s.ogg" type="audio/ogg">
   <source src="s.aac" type="audio/mp4">
   HTML5 audio not supported
</audio>
```

The preceding HTML5 <audio> tag specifies a file in multiple formats,
and when you launch a Web page with this tag, your browser will start from the
first <source> element in order to find a format that it recognizes and then
play the audio file that is specified in the src attribute.

In addition, you can also programmatically control the <audio> tag using
JavaScript code, and Listing 6.2 displays the contents of an HTML5 Web page
with an <audio> tag and some error-handling JavaScript code.

LISTING 6.2 HTML5Audio2.html

```
<!DOCTYPE HTML>
<html lang="en">
 <head>
  <meta charset="utf-8" />
  <title>HTML5 Audio With Error Detection</title>

  <script>
   function ReportError(e) {
    switch (e.target.error.code) {
      case e.target.error.MEDIA_ERR_ABORTED:
        alert("User aborted the playback.");
        break;
```

```
      case e.target.error.MEDIA_ERR_NETWORK:
        alert("Network error.");
        break;
      case e.target.error.MEDIA_ERR_DECODE:
        alert("The File is Corrupted.");
        break;
      case e.target.error.MEDIA_ERR_SRC_NOT_SUPPORTED:
        alert("Unsupported Format or File not Found.");
        break;
      default:
        alert("An Unknown Error Occurred.");
        break;
    }
  }
 </script>
</head>

<body>
 <h1>HTML 5 Audio</h1>
 <audio controls onerror="ReportError(event)" src="Japanese1.m4a">
 </audio>
</body>
</html>
```

Listing 6.2 contains the JavaScript function `ReportError()` that is invoked when an error occurs while playing the audio file in this `<audio>` element:

```
<audio controls onerror="ReportError(event)" src="Japanese1.m4a">
```

The `ReportError()` function contains a `switch` statement that displays an alert when any of the following errors occurs:

```
MEDIA_ERR_ABORTED
MEDIA_ERR_NETWORK
MEDIA_ERR_DECODE
MEDIA_ERR_SRC_NOT_SUPPORTED
```

Some interesting audio demos in Google Chrome are here:

http://chromium.googlecode.com/svn/trunk/samples/audio/index.html

If you want to learn more about HTML5 `Audio` features, you can read the W3C `Audio` specification here:

https://dvcs.w3.org/hg/audio/raw-file/tip/webaudio/specification.html

THE HTML5 `<VIDEO>` ELEMENT

The HTML5 `<video>` tag can be as minimal as the HTML5 `<audio>` tag, and its syntax looks like this:

```
<video>
  <source type="video/mp4" src="filename">
</video>
```

As you might have surmised, you can also include multiple `<source>` elements in the HTML5 `<video>` element, as shown here:

```
<video poster="MyVideo.gif" controls>
  <source src='MyVideo.mp4'
          type='video/mp4; codecs="avc1.4D401E, mp4a.40.2"'>
  <source src='MyVideo.ogv'
          type='video/ogg; codecs="theora, vorbis"'>
  <source src='MyVideo.webm'
          type='video/webm; codecs="vp8.0, vorbis"'>
 <p>Your browser does not support the video element</p>
</video>
```

The current HTML5 specification does not specify any video formats whose support is required, but the following video formats are commonly supported in modern browsers:

- MP4 (MPEG4 files with H.264 video codec and AAC audio codec).
- Ogg (Ogg files with Theodora video codec and Vorbis audio codec) are commonly supported in modern browsers. On mobile devices, the iPhone simulator supports MP4, Android hardware support h.264, and the Android simulator supports Ogg Vorbis.
- WebM or VP8, which is a royalty-free open audio-video compression format with the .WebM extension (currently has a low adoption rate).

On the mobile side of things, both iOS and Android only support MP4 video.

Listing 6.3 displays the contents of `HTML5Video1.html` that illustrates how to play a video file in an HTML5 Web page.

LISTING 6.3 HTML5Video1.html

```
<!DOCTYPE HTML>
<html>
<head>
  <meta charset="utf-8" />
  <title>Working With HTML5 Video</title>
</head>

<body>
  <video width="800" height="500"
         controls poster="sample1.png" id="video1">
    <source src="Rectangle1.mov" type="video/mp4">
    <source src="Rectangle1.ogg" type="video/ogg">
  </video>
</body>
</html>
```

Listing 6.3 contains some boilerplate code, along with an HTML5 `<video>` element whose attributes are similar to the HTML5 `<audio>` element. Note that the HTML5 `<video>` element in Listing 6.3 specifies two `<source>` elements whose `src` attribute references the same video file, but in two different formats. Browsers handle an HTML5 <video> element in a similar fashion as an HTML5 <audio> element: when you launch an HTML5 Web page with an HTML5 <video> element in a browser, your browser will play the first video whose format is recognized by the browser.

Note: You need to provide a video file for Listing 6.3 in order to see the video functionality.

In a previous section, you saw how to use JavaScript to bind to audio elements, and you can do the same thing with video elements (and also include a custom progress bar).

Listing 6.4 displays the contents of HTML5Video2.html that illustrates how to play a video file in an HTML5 Web page that contains error-handling code in JavaScript.

LISTING 6.4 HTML5Video2.html

```
<!DOCTYPE HTML>
<html lang="en">
<head>
 <meta charset="utf-8" />
 <title></title>

 <style>
   /* selectors for playing and paused */
   .paused  { }
   .playing { }
 </style>

 <script>
  function init() {
     var video = document.getElementById("video1");
     var toggle = document.getElementById("toggle1");

     toggle.onclick = function() {
       if (video.paused) {
         video.play();
         toggle.className="playing"
       } else {
         video.pause();
         toggle.className="paused"
       }
     }
  }
 </script>
</head>

<body onload="init()">
 <figure>
   <video src="media/video1.webm" controls autoplay
          id="video1" width="400" height="300"
          data-description="Sample Video">
     This browser does not support the video tag </video>
   <legend>Sample Video</legend>
 </figure>
```

```
<div id="toggle1"> </div>
</body>
</html>
```

Listing 6.4 contains a JavaScript `init()` method that is executed when the Web page is loaded into a browser, and this method contains JavaScript code that handles the play and pause events for the video element, as shown here:

```
var video = document.getElementById("video1");
var toggle = document.getElementById("toggle1");

toggle.onclick = function() {
    if (video.paused) {
      video.play();
      toggle.className="playing"
    } else {
      video.pause();
      toggle.className="paused"
    }
}
```

Listing 6.4 also contains boilerplate code and an HTML5 `<video>` element that specifies a video file and also video controls that users can use to control the video, as shown here:

```
<video src="media/video1.webm" controls autoplay
      id="video1" width="400" height="300"
      data-description="Sample Video">
   This browser does not support the video tag
</video>
```

As you can see, the CSS selectors `playing` and `paused` are currently empty; their contents would contain properties that perform your styling effects.

Note: You need to provide a video file for Listing 6.4 in order to see the video functionality.

A useful link with information about the status of HTML5 video and a link to an interesting Website for HTML5 video support are here:

http://www.longtailvideo.com/html5/
http://videojs.com/

The HTML `<video>` element also supports the `canPlayType()` method that enables you to determine programmatically how likely your browser can play different video types. This method returns "probably," "maybe," or an empty string.

Listing 6.5 displays the contents of `HTML5Video3.html` that illustrates how to check browser support for different video types.

LISTING 6.5 HTML5Video3.html

```
<!DOCTYPE HTML>
<html lang="en">
<head>
```

```
<meta charset="utf-8" />
<title>Detecting Video Support</title>

<script>
 var videoTypes = ['video/ogg; codecs="theora, vorbis"',
                    'video/ogg',
                    'video/mp4',
                    'video/ogv',
                    'video/webm'
                   ];

 function init() {
   var video = document.getElementById("video1");
   var canPlay, videoType;

   for(var v=0; v<videoTypes.length; v++) {
      videoType = videoTypes[v];
      canPlay = video.canPlayType(videoType);

console.log("Type: "+videoType+" Can Play: "+canPlay);
   }
 }
 </script>
</head>

<body onload="init()">
 <figure>
   <video src="media/HelloWorld.ogg" controls autoplay
          id="video1" width="400" height="300"
          data-description="Sample Video">
     This browser does not support the video tag </video>
   <legend>Sample Video</legend>
 </figure>
</body>
</html>
```

Listing 6.5 contains a JavaScript array `videoTypes` that specifies information about various video formats, and the first entry is the most detailed information. The JavaScript function `init()` is invoked when the Web page is loaded into a browser, and it contains a loop that iterates through the array of video formats and checks which ones are supported by your browser.

If you launch a Chrome browser (version 19) on a Macbook, you will see the following output in the console:

```
Type: video/ogg; codecs="theora, vorbis" Can Play: probably
Type: video/ogg Can Play: maybe
Type: video/mp4 Can Play: maybe
Type: video/ogv Can Play:
Type: video/webm Can Play: maybe
```

Notice that the first line specifies the codecs, and the browser has determined that it can probably play the given video type, whereas the second line is "maybe" because the codecs are not specified.

A Website that contains useful information regarding video support in HTML5 (on mobile as well as desktop) is here:

http://www.longtailvideo.com/html5

For a detailed analysis of some video-related performance results regarding Safari on iOS, Steve Souders provides a blog post here:

http://www.stevesouders.com/blog/2013/04/21/html5-video-bytes-on-ios/

Steve Souders currently works at Google and he is the author of two performance-related books.

In addition, a "deep dive" video with mobile performance tips by Ilya Grigorik (also a Google employee) is here:

https://plus.google.com/u/0/+IlyaGrigorik/posts/Ev7RHf7GGTk?cfem=1

Popcorn.js: HTML5 Media Framework

`Popcorn.js` is part of the Mozilla Popcorn project, and it is a JavaScript-based HTML5 media framework for creating time-based interactive media. The `Popcorn.js` homepage and the download link are here:

http://popcornjs.org
http://popcornjs.org/download

`Popcorn.js` consists of a core JavaScript library (available as a separate download) and plugins. You can also create a customized download of `Popcorn.js`, along with minified and debug versions. Navigate to the homepage for additional information, as well as documentation and a video with a demonstration of `Popcorn.js`.

HTML5 <VIDEO> AND WEB CAMERA SUPPORT

You can use the HTML5 `<video>` tag for real-time camera support via the `getUserMedia()` API, which is currently "work in progress." This functionality is already available in Opera (see the link below). As this book goes to print, this functionality has appeared in the Chrome "nightly" builds, which is accessible via the `getUserMedia()` API.

For other useful information regarding HTML5 video, visit this Website:

http://html5video.org/

Listing 6.6 displays the contents of `WebCamera1.html` that illustrates how to activate a camera in a browser (currently this works only in Opera).

LISTING 6.6: WebCamera1.html

```
<!DOCTYPE HTML>
<html>
<head>
 <meta charset="utf-8" />
```

```
  <title>HTML5 Web Camera</title>
</head>

<body>
<h1>Web camera display demo</h1>
<video autoplay></video>
<script>
 var video = document.getElementsByTagName('video')[0],
     heading = document.getElementsByTagName('h1')[0];

if(navigator.getUserMedia) {
  navigator.getUserMedia('video', successCallback, errorCallback);
  function successCallback( stream ) {
    video.src = stream;
  }
  function errorCallback( error ) {
    heading.textContent =
        "An error occurred: [CODE " + error.code + "]";
  }
} else {
  heading.textContent =
      "Native web camera streaming is not supported in this
browser";
}
</script>
</body>
</html>
```

Listing 6.6 checks for the presence of `navigator.getUserMedia`, and if it does exist, then an invocation of the `getUserMedia()` method searches for the HTML5 `<video>` tag and provides both success and failure JavaScript callback functions, as shown here:

```
navigator.getUserMedia('video', successCallback, errorCallback);
```

An Opera build that provides Web camera support for Linux, Mac, Windows, and Android is available for download here:

http://dev.opera.com/articles/view/labs-more-fun-using-the-web-with-getusermedia-and-native-pages/

Although the HTML5 technologies Navigation Timing, RDFa, and Selectors have CR status, they are not discussed in this book.

BATTERY API (DAP)

This section of the chapter contains a set of HTML5 APIs that have Candidate Recommendation status.

The Battery API is maintained by the DAP (Device APIs) working group. This set of APIs provides information about the battery status of the hosting device, and this API as Candidate Recommendation (CR) status. The following simple code snippet writes the battery level to the console each time the level changes:

```
navigator.battery.onlevelchange = function () {
  console.log(navigator.battery.level);
};
```

Listing 6.7 displays the contents of the HTML Web page `Battery.html` that illustrates how to use the Battery API in a Web page.

LISTING 6.7 Battery.html

```
<!DOCTYPE html>
<html>
<head>
 <meta charset="utf-8" />
 <title>Battery Status API Example</title>

 <script>
  var battery = navigator.battery;

  if(battery != null) {
      battery.onchargingchange = function () {
        document.querySelector('#charging').textContent =
          battery.charging ? 'charging' : 'not charging';
        };

      battery.onlevelchange = function () {
        document.querySelector('#level').textContent =
                                        battery.level;
        };

      battery.ondischargingtimechange = function () {
        document.querySelector('#dischargingTime').textContent =
                                battery.dischargingTime / 60;
        };
  } else {
      console.log("Battery not Supported in this Browser");
  }
 </script>
</head>

<body>
  <div id="charging">(charging state unknown)</div>
  <div id="level">(battery level unknown)</div>
  <div id="dischargingTime">(discharging time unknown)</div>
</body>
</html>
```

Listing 6.7 contains JavaScript code that first ensures that `navigator.battery` is non-null, and then defines three straightforward JavaScript functions that handle change-related battery events: `onchargingchange`, `onlevelchange`, and `ondischargingtimechange`. The JavaScript functions simply update the contents of an associated `<div>` element that is located in the `<body>` element of Listing 6.7.

You can find additional information about the Battery API in the W3C specification:

http://www.w3.org/TR/battery-status

VIBRATION API (DAP)

The Vibration API (maintained by the DAP working group) defines an API that provides access to the vibration mechanism of a hosting device. The Vibration API consists of a single method `vibrate()` whose implementation must run the algorithm for processing vibration patterns (see link below for details).

In the following example, the device vibrates for 1 second:

```
// vibrate for 1 second
navigator.vibrate(1000);
```

Using the following code snippet to cause a device to vibrate for 1 second, stop vibration for 0.5 seconds, and vibrate again for 2 seconds:

```
navigator.vibrate([1000, 500, 2000]);
```

Cancel any existing vibrations:

```
navigator.vibrate(0);
```

Cancel any existing vibrations:

```
navigator.vibrate([]);
```

For additional information, navigate to the W3C Vibration API (currently a working draft):

http://www.w3.org/TR/vibration/

HTML5 APIS IN W3C WORKING DRAFT STATUS (WD)

The HTML5 technologies in this section (listed in alphabetical order) currently have a "Working Draft" status. IndexedDB has WD status and it is discussed in Chapter 1, so we will not repeat that content here. In addition, the following HTML5 technologies also have WD status but they are not discussed in this chapter:

- Media Capture
- RDFa
- Touch Events

AUDIO PROCESSING

The W3C Audio Processing API introduces two APIs: Google's Web Audio API specification and Mozilla's MediaStream Processing API specification. The code sample in this section illustrates how to use the audio APIs for Mozilla, which means that you need to launch the HTML Web page in Firefox.

In Chapter 1, you saw an example of the HTML5 <audio> element, and in this section you will see a code sample that uses the Web Audio APIs, which enable you to access low-level data. The code sample shows you how to play an audio file and then render a set of rectangles that are rendered along a sine wave that represents the amplitude of the sounds in the audio file.

The code sample in this section works in Firefox and Safari 6, and undoubtedly will be available in Chrome in the future. This code sample in Listing 6.11 is one of the few code samples in this book that are not WebKit-based code samples because the visual effects are interesting and worth including in this book.

Listing 6.8 displays the contents of the HTML Web page WebAudio1.html that illustrates how to use the Web Audio API in an HTML Web page.

LISTING 6.8 WebAudio1.html

```
<!DOCTYPE html>
<html lang="en">
<head>
  <meta charset="utf-8" />
  <title>HTML5 Audio Visualization</title>
</head>

<body>
  <h2>Audio Sampling Example</h2>
  <audio tabloop="0" src="HelloWorld.ogg" controls="controls">
  </audio>

  <div>
    <canvas width="512" height="200" style="background-color:yellow;">
    </canvas>

    <canvas width="512" height="200" style="background-color:yellow;">
    </canvas>

    <canvas width="512" height="200" style="background-color:yellow;">
    </canvas>

    <canvas width="512" height="200" style="background-color:yellow;">
    </canvas>
  </div>

  <script>
    var sampleCount = 512, rectWidth=sampleCount, rectHeight=200;
    var barWidth = 10, barHeight = 0, deltaX1 = 2, deltaX4 = 5;
    var x1, y1, x2, y2, x3, y3, x4, y4, index, loop = 0;
    var fillColors = ["#f00", "#ff0", "#00f", "#0ff", "#804"];
    var smallWidth = 10, smallHeight = 40, fbLength, channels;
```

```
var audio   = document.getElementsByTagName("audio")[0];
var canvas1 = document.getElementsByTagName("canvas")[0];
var canvas2 = document.getElementsByTagName("canvas")[1];
var canvas3 = document.getElementsByTagName("canvas")[2];
var canvas4 = document.getElementsByTagName("canvas")[3];

var context1 = canvas1.getContext('2d');
var context2 = canvas2.getContext('2d');
var context3 = canvas3.getContext('2d');
var context4 = canvas4.getContext('2d');

context1.lineWidth = 2; context1.strokeStyle = "#FFFFFF";
context2.lineWidth = 4; context2.strokeStyle = "#FFFFFF";
context3.lineWidth = 6; context3.strokeStyle = "#FFFFFF";
context4.lineWidth = 1; context4.strokeStyle = "#FFFFFF";

audio.addEventListener("MozAudioAvailable", writeSamples, false);
audio.addEventListener("loadedmetadata", getMetadata, false);

function getMetadata() {
  channels = audio.mozChannels;
  fbLength = audio.mozFrameBufferLength;
}

// Render the waveforms
function writeSamples (event) {
  var data = event.frameBuffer;
  var step = (fbLength / channels) / sampleCount;

  if(loop % 4 == 0) {
    // clear the canvas:
    context1.fillRect(0, 0, rectWidth, rectHeight);

    context1.beginPath();
    for(var x=1; x<sampleCount; x+= deltaX1){
      barHeight = 2*data[x*step]*rectHeight/2;
      context1.fillStyle = fillColors[x % fillColors.
length];
      context1.fillRect(x, rectHeight/2-barHeight,
                           barWidth, barHeight);
    }
  } else if(loop % 4 == 1) {
    context2.strokeStyle = fillColors[loop % fillColors.
length];

    context2.beginPath();
    context2.moveTo(0, rectHeight/2-data[0]*rectHeight/2);

    for(var x=1; x<sampleCount; x++){
      context2.lineTo(x, rectHeight/2-data[x*step]*rectHeight/2);
    }
    context2.stroke();
  } else if(loop % 4 == 2) {
    index = Math.floor(Math.random()*5);

    x1 = (8*loop) % sampleCount;
    y1 = rectHeight  - (loop % rectHeight);
```

```
          x2 = sampleCount - (loop % sampleCount);
          y2 = rectHeight/2-data[step*(sampleCount-
1)]*rectHeight/2;
          x3 = sampleCount/2;
          y3 = rectHeight/2-data[step*sampleCount/2]*rectHeight/2;

          context3.strokeStyle = fillColors[index % fillColors.length];
          context3.fillStyle = fillColors[(index+1)%fillColors.length];
          context3.moveTo(x1, y1);
          context3.quadraticCurveTo(x2, y2, x3, y3);

          context3.fill();
          context3.stroke();
        } else {
          context4.strokeStyle = fillColors[loop % fillColors.
length];

          context4.beginPath();
          context4.moveTo(0, rectHeight/2-data[0]*rectHeight/2);

          for(var x=1; x<sampleCount; x+=deltaX4){
            context4.strokeRect(
                          x, rectHeight/2-
data[x*step]*rectHeight/2,
                          smallWidth, smallHeight);
          }
          context4.stroke();
        }

        ++loop;
      }
    </script>
  </body>
<html>
```

The graphics effects in Listing 6.8 involve a sine-based bar chart, squiggly lines, a set of Bezier curves, and then another set of "fuzzy" random squiggly lines.

Listing 6.8 contains four HTML5 <canvas> elements that are used for rendering graphics that are based on the amplitude of the sounds in the audio file. The JavaScript function writeSamples() uses the value of the expression loop%4 to select one of the four HTML5 <canvas> element and then render some graphics in that element. Although this rendering is done in a "round-robin" fashion, the speed of code execution creates the illusion that the rendering effects is performed simultaneously in all four <canvas> elements.

The first part of the code initializes a channels variable (which is an object) and the variable fbLength (which is the length of the frame buffer of the audio), so that we capture the amplitude of the audio signal that we are sampling, as shown here:

```
function getMetadata() {
  channels = audio.mozChannels;
  fbLength = audio.mozFrameBufferLength;
}
```

The actual graphics images are easy to render, as you can see from the following block of code that computes the height of bar elements based on the values of the audio that are contained in the `data` array (which is pre-populated for us), and then renders a sine-based bar chart:

```
for(var x=1; x<sampleCount; x+= deltaX1){
  barHeight = 2*data[x*step]*rectHeight/2;
  context1.fillStyle = fillColors[x % fillColors.length];
  context1.fillRect(x, rectHeight/2-barHeight,
                    barWidth, barHeight);
}
```

Figure 6.1 displays the result of rendering Listing 6.8 in a Chrome browser on a Macbook.

Note that the code in Listing 6.8 is based on a code sample from this Website:

http://html5videoguide.net/ chapter8.html

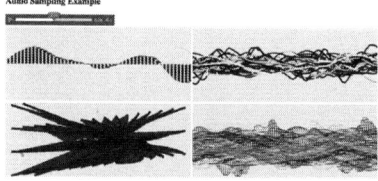

FIGURE 6.1 Converting Audio Waves into Graphics on a Macbook.

Chris Wilson created a Website that enables you to drag-and-drop components onto a Web page in order to apply various effects to audio files, and its homepage is here:

https://webaudioplayground.appspot.com/

Chris Wilson is also a co-editor of the W3C Web MIDI API specification:

https://dvcs.w3.org/hg/audio/raw-file/tip/midi/specification.html

Other interesting Web Audio code samples are here:

http://updates.html5rocks.com/2012/02/HTML5-audio-and-the-Web-Audio-API-are-BFFs
http://www.html5audio.org/2012/05/new-google-doodle-uses-web-audio-api.html
http://www.html5rocks.com/en/tutorials/webaudio/positional_audio/
http://chromium.googlecode.com/svn/trunk/samples/audio/index.html
http://jeromeetienne.github.com/slides/webaudioapi/#1
https://bleedinghtml5.appspot.com/#1

SUMMARY

This chapter provided an overview of several HTML5-related techniques for managing and persisting user-provided data using HTML5 `Forms`. In this chapter, you learned how to use the HTML5 `<audio>` and `<video>` elements, and you also learned about some of the Web Audio APIs.

CHAPTER 7

DESIGN, DEBUG, AND TEST MOBILE APPS

The goal of this chapter is to provide you with some guidelines for designing good HTML5 mobile applications, along with tools for debugging and testing those mobile applications. This chapter discusses aspects of the UI experience, and how to create aesthetically appealing mobile Web applications. In addition, this chapter covers some of the toolkits that can help you support the desired functionality without sacrificing important design considerations. Some of the sections in this chapter rely on CSS3 media queries from Chapter 4, so you might need to review the relevant sections in that chapter prior to reading some of the sections in this chapter.

The first part of this chapter discusses some of the major aspects of the mobile metaphor, which is touch-oriented instead of mouse-oriented. The second part of this chapter delves into debugging tools that are available for mobile Web applications. You will learn about using `console.log()` statements that are part of your HTML5 Web pages, which is the simplest technique for debugging your code. You will also learn two JavaScript coding techniques that can help you pinpoint JavaScript errors in your HTML5 Web pages. The final portion of this chapter discusses performance considerations for mobile Web applications.

WHAT IS GOOD MOBILE DESIGN?

The answer to this simple question is more complex than you might think, but there are some guidelines to help you make design decisions for hybrid HTML5 mobile applications (and also native applications, but those are outside the scope of this book).

The next several sections identify important factors and then discuss toolkits or provide code snippets that can help you implement the desired functionality.

IMPORTANT FACETS OF MOBILE WEB DESIGN

Some of the important considerations for designing hybrid HTML5 mobile applications are here:

- a touch-oriented design (not mouse-oriented)
- improving response times of user gestures
- detecting different screen sizes (especially for Android devices)
- resizing assets (such as images)
- determining the content of a Web page

Instead of handling mouse clicks, mobile Web applications handle touch-related events (single tap and multiple taps) and user gestures (swipe, flick, pan, and so forth).

Fortunately, jQuery Mobile (discussed in Chapter 8) provides a virtualization of events that takes care of mouse events and touch events through a single set of APIs. This virtualization simplifies your code. You only need to handle one set of events.

A TOUCH-ORIENTED DESIGN

You might think that you can accomplish this goal simply by replacing all mouse-related events with their touch-related counterparts. Although this is a good starting point, there are several caveats to this approach. First, there is no touch event that is the counterpart for a mouse-based hover event. Consequently, CSS stylesheets with selectors of the type #myDiv:hover will work correctly on laptops and desktops, but they do not work correctly on mobile devices.

Second, when users touch a mobile screen with one of their fingers, the second gesture could be one of the following:

- touch up
- touch hold
- touch move
- swipe gesture

For this reason, there is a delay (roughly 300 milliseconds) to allow for a second event. The first event (touch down) can be combined with the second event to determine the correct user gesture. However, this delay can affect the perceived responsiveness of a mobile Web application. Fortunately, there are JavaScript toolkits that improve touch-related responsiveness of mobile Web applications, which is the topic of the next section.

IMPROVING RESPONSE TIMES OF USER GESTURES

There are several toolkits for eliminating the 300 millisecond delay between the first touch event and the second touch event. The first JavaScript toolkit with nice touch-related functionality is `fastclick.js`, and its home page is here:

https://github.com/ftlabs/fastclick

Mobile browsers wait about 300 ms after an initial tap event in order to determine if users will perform a double tap. Since FastClick eliminates the 300 ms delay between a physical tap and the firing of a click event on mobile browsers, mobile applications feel more responsive when the delay is eliminated.

Listing 7.1 displays the contents of the HTML5 Web page `FastClick1.html` that illustrates how to use `fastclick.js` in a Web page.

LISTING 7.1 FastClick1.html

```html
<html>
<head>
  <meta charset="utf-8">
  <script src='/path/to/fastclick.js'></script>
</head>

<body>
  <script>
    window.addEventListener('load', function() {
        FastClick.attach(document.body);
    }, false);
  </script>
</body>
</html>
```

You can also use `fastclick.js` with mobile Web applications that use jQuery Mobile, and a detailed description is provided here:

http://forum.jquery.com/topic/how-to-remove-the-300ms-delay-when-clicking-on-a-link-in-jquery-mobile

The second JavaScript toolkit is `energize.js`, and its homepage is here:

https://github.com/davidcalhoun/energize.js

The author of this toolkit mentions that `energize.js` is a "work in progress" yet functional in terms of its goals.

Make sure that you include `energize.js` before any other code that handles with click events (including any libraries and frameworks) because `energize.js` fires simulated click events and also needs to suppress the "ghost click," which is the real click event that is fired later.

This Website also points out that binding to the `ontouchend` event does not always handle user gestures in the desired fashion. For example, if users touch an element in order to scroll that element, then the `ontouchend` fires at the end of the scroll event. In this scenario, a click event is fired when the user intended to scroll an element (which is not the desired behavior).

DETECTING SCREEN SIZES OF MOBILE DEVICES

Mobile applications that run on multiple mobile devices need to detect different screen sizes on those mobile devices. Smart phones tend to have the following screen sizes (expressed as width × height):

- 128 × 160 pixels (Phones such as the Fujitsu DoCoMo F504i)
- 176 × 220 pixels (Phones such as the HP iPAQ 510)
- 240 × 320 pixels (Smart phones such as Blackberry 8100 or the HTC Elf)
- 320 × 480 pixels (PDAs such as the Garmin-AsusA50 or the Palm Pre)

Tablets generally have dimensions that vary from 1024–1280 pixels for their height, and 600–800 pixels for their width.

There are at least two common techniques for detecting screen sizes. The first technique (discussed in Chapter 4) involves CSS3 media queries to load different CSS stylesheets for different screen widths. The second technique (also in Chapter 4) is to use JavaScript to set different CSS properties for different screen sizes. Now that you have an understanding of how to detect different screen sizes, you can explore techniques for resizing assets so that they render appropriately on different devices, which is the topic of the next section.

RESIZING ASSETS IN MOBILE WEB APPLICATIONS

When you place assets (such as PNG files) on an HTML5 Web page in a mobile Web application, you need to decide how to handle the following situations for your mobile Web application:

- switching from portrait to landscape (or vice versa)
- deploying to mobile devices with different screen sizes
- resizing text strings and text areas
- scaling non-binary images (such as SVG)

You need to address the preceding situations whenever you create an HTML5 Web page that includes not only PNG files, but also other types of assets, such as embedded SVG documents or HTML5 `<canvas>` elements.

In the case of rendering text strings, how do you determine the correct font size? Even if you use em for the unit of measure, you don't know the DPI resolution of a particular device. Of course, you could make an educated guess and decide that text will be rendered with `14em` for a mobile phone and `16em` for a tablet (or phablet), but the increasing variety of screens with different DPIs means that you can't guarantee that your choice will be correct in all cases.

In the case of SVG documents that are embedded in an HTML5 Web page, you can use a CSS-based technique for automatically resizing the contents of SVG documents in an HTML5 Web page with this code snippet:

```
<div style="background-size: contain">
```

A detailed description of this technique is here:

https://developer.mozilla.org/en-US/docs/Web/CSS/background-size

DETERMINING THE CONTENT LAYOUT FOR MOBILE WEB PAGES

Some design considerations for determining the content of a Web page are here:

- provide a single column of text for smart phones
- remove extra links and content
- remove items sidebars/footers
- avoid absolute sizes
- set wrapper widths to percentages
- set paragraphs to display block

Keep in mind that the preceding points are guidelines, and not absolute rules. For example, some smart phones in landscape mode can accommodate two columns, depending on the width of the columns, and many tablets can display two columns in portrait mode. Some people recommend that you reduce the amount of scrolling that is required in a screen, but many users are accustomed to frequent scrolling on a mobile device (especially on smart phones). When in doubt, create two (or possible more) layouts and get feedback from users to determine which layout might have greater appeal to a broad audience. If you still cannot decide which layout design is best for your purposes, perhaps you can benefit from "A/B testing," which is described here:

http://en.wikipedia.org/wiki/A/B_testing

MOBILE DESIGN FOR HTML WEB PAGES

There are several approaches to designing HTML Web pages for mobile devices, including "mobile first," "mobile only," and using a separate domain for mobile applications.

A "mobile first" approach ensures that an HTML Web page will render correctly on a mobile device. However, you need to take into account different screen sizes among mobile devices, such as smart phones, "phablets," and tablets. This detail is particularly evident about Android mobile devices (and to a less extent it's true for iOS devices).

A "mobile only" approach still requires you to take into account different screen sizes on mobile devices, but in this scenario you do not need to contend with HTML Web pages for laptops or desktops. Keep in mind that this approach is far from trivial: it can involve a combination of client (or server) templates, local data stores, and efficient view-model binding that are provided by toolkits such as BackboneJS. Another point to consider is whether or not you can leverage NoSQL datastores.

A third approach is to use separate domains for mobile versus desktop Web pages. If you are developing thin mobile Web applications (i.e., Web pages that are hosted on a server and accessed by various device types), this approach provides several advantages. First, this makes your mobile site easier to find. Second, you can advertise the mobile URL separately from the URL for desktop devices. Third, users can switch between the "regular" Website and the mobile Website simply by changing the domain. Fourth, the code logic for detecting mobile users (and then sending them to a separate domain) is simpler than making modifications to CSS stylesheets.

Now that you have an overview of design considerations for mobile Web pages, let's take a look at an example of styling mobile forms, which is the topic of the next section.

HIGH-LEVEL VIEW OF STYLING MOBILE FORMS

When you render a mobile form, there are high-level techniques (such as how to display input fields) as well as techniques that are specific in nature (such as indicating required fields).

The following list contains some high-level techniques for rendering mobile forms:

- use semantic markup
- use a single column to display input fields (for smart phones)
- deciding on label alignment (left or top)
- grouping/chunking input fields
- tooltips or information bubbles
- displaying error messages
- appropriate field width
- suitable color scheme
- tabs instead of radio buttons
- handling long drop-down lists (use predictive search or links)
- primary and secondary buttons
- spacing between input elements
- pop-up menu controls
- voice input

Notice that there is no "reduce scrolling" in the previous list: users are accustomed to scrolling on smart phones and tablets. In addition, a single-column display was more important for smaller smart phones, but some smart phones can display two columns in landscape mode, and tablets are even more accommodating in terms of multiple columns of text.

If you render text in a left-to-right direction, then left-aligned labels enable you to place more input fields in a screen, and they are also easier to scan during field input, but they don't work well with long input fields. Top-aligned labels have the opposite advantages and disadvantages of left-aligned labels. Yet another technique is use inline labeling, which essentially means that the "text prompt" for the input field provides a suggestion for the type of data that is expected.

SPECIFIC TECHNIQUES FOR STYLING MOBILE FORMS

In addition to the design techniques that are listed in the previous section, you can use some or all of these specific techniques:

- use CSS to style input fields differently
- provide labels for input fields
- specify keyboard types for input fields
- provide default or suggested values for input fields
- use constraints for numeric fields
- indicate required fields
- validate each field after user input
- password masking
- field zoom

The following subsections provide additional details for some of the bullet items in the preceding list.

Use CSS to Style Input Fields Differently

There are two steps involved. The first step is to apply the default styling and then apply your own styling rules. The second step is to use the [type=] attribute selector to apply different styles to different input fields.

As a specific example, you can use the -webkit-appearance property (available in WebKit browsers) to remove the default styling for all input elements, as shown here:

```
input, textarea, select {
   -webkit-appearance: none;
}
```

Next, specify your own CSS styles that depend on the type of input field, as outlined here:

```
input[type=checkbox]
   /* specify styles for checkbox */
}

input[type=radio] {
   /* specify styles for radio */
}

input[type=textarea] {
   /* specify styles for textarea */
}
```

You can use the preceding example as a guideline for defining CSS selectors to change the appearance of other HTML elements in your Web pages.

Specify Keyboard Types for Input Fields

HTML5 introduced the following new properties for the type attribute for input elements:

```
an email address: type='email'
a website address: type='url'
telephone number: type='tel'
```

The preceding types only work on mobile browsers (nothing will happen in a laptop or desktop browser).

The following example shows you how to specify different keyboards for input fields:

```
<form id="form1" name="form1" method="post" action="">
<label for="name">Name:</label><input name="name" id="name"
type="text" /><br />
<label for="email">Email:</label><input name="email" id="email"
type="email" /><br />
<label for="phone">Phone:</label><input name="phone" id="phone"
type="tel" /><br />
<input name="submit" type="button" value="Submit" />
</form>
```

Different Countries and Languages

There are several points to keep in mind when you create applications for different countries and languages:

• different phone formats in different countries
• left-to-right versus right-to-left text input
• culturally appropriate content

If you intend to publish Android applications that support multiple languages, the following link provides useful information:

http://developer.vodafone.com/how-support-multiple-languages-android/

If you intend to publish iOS applications that support multiple countries and languages, Apple provides extensive information here:

https://developer.apple.com/internationalization/

The details of creating internationalized iOS mobile applications (such as how to create additional string resources) are here:

http://www.slideshare.net/cxpartners/web-and-mobile-forms-design-userfriendly-2010-workshop

DESIGN-RELATED TOOLS AND ONLINE PATTERNS

Balsamiq is an online design tool, and its homepage is here:

http://www.balsamiq.com/

`Balsamic Mockups` is a tool for rapidly creating wireframes, designed to reproduce the experience of sketching interfaces on a whiteboard. Because these mockups are on your computer, you can share them quickly and easily with other people.

Another toolkit for creating wireframes is `justinmind`, and its homepage is here:

http://justinmind.com

Both of the preceding tools are free to use, and they have videos that illustrate how to use them.

Two Websites that provide a collection of design patterns (the second is purely for mobile) are here:

http://pttrns.com
http://mobile-patterns.com

Perform an Internet search for other design tools and design patterns.

WORKING WITH FONT SIZES AND UNITS OF MEASURE

If you have already worked with CSS stylesheets, then you are already familiar with different units that are available for expressing font sizes for text in HTML5 Web pages. Several units are available, including `em`, `rem`, `px`, `pt`, and `%`.

The relationship among these units is as follows:

```
1em = 12pt = 16px = 100%
```

Pixel units (`px`) are very common in Web pages (especially for desktops and laptops), and they can vary in terms of their resolution and their DPI (dots per inch). Pixel units are virtual screen pixels rather than physical pixels. One point to keep in mind is that the pixel unit does not scale correctly for visually impaired readers.

You can use the `px` unit for text, images, borders, rounded corners, and drop shadows. However, if you are building a fluid layout that uses relative sizes, it's probably better to use the `em` unit or the `%` unit for text.

The `em` unit is becoming more popular, especially on mobile devices, because this unit is well suited for scaling a Web page. Unlike the `px` unit, the `em` unit is relative to its parent element in a Web page. It might be helpful to think of the `px` unit as "global" whereas the `em` unit is "local."

One useful technique is to specify the value `62.5%` for the `<body>` element. Because 62.5% equals the fraction `5/8`, the product of `16px` and `5/8` is `10px`. The value `10px` is a convenient "base point" for performing conversions quickly and easily between `px` units and `em` units in CSS selectors. For example, `1.5em` is `15px`, `2em` is `20px`, `2.5em` is `25px`, and so forth. In case you need help in performing conversions, an online `em` calculator is here:

http://riddle.pl/emcalc/
http://www.ready.mobi/launch.jsp?locale=en_EN

Additional useful information is here:

http://www.w3.org/QA/Tips/font-size

TWITTER BOOTSTRAP 2.0

Twitter Bootstrap is currently the most downloaded repository in github, which reflects its popularity. In case you didn't already know, Twitter Bootstrap provides simple and flexible HTML, CSS, and JavaScript for user interface components and interactions. Currently, Twitter Bootstrap is the most watched and forked repository in GitHub, and its homepage is here:

http://twitter.github.com/bootstrap/
http://blog.getbootstrap.com/
http://www.queness.com/post/11632/18-useful-twitter-boostrap-goodies-you-should-know

Bootstrap was designed primarily as a style guide to document best practices, and also to be for people diverse skill levels. Bootstrap supports new HTML5 elements and syntax, and you can use Bootstrap as a complete kit or to start something more complex.

Bootstrap was initially created for modern browsers, but it has expanded its support to include all major browsers (including IE7). In addition, Bootstrap 2 supports tablets and smart phones.

Bootstrap 2 supports tablets and smart phones, and its responsive design means that its components are scaled according to a range of resolutions and devices, thereby providing a consistent experience. Moreover, Bootstrap provides custom-built jQuery plugins, and it's built on top of the LESS toolkit. Some features of Bootstrap 2.0 are tooltips, styled stateful buttons, more table and form styling, and an improved structure for its CSS source code (multiple files instead of a single monolithic file).

Bootstrap handles layouts and provides various components, as well as support for popovers, dropdown menus, carousel content, modals, and other functionality. In addition, Bootstrap 2.0 supports responsive design for mobile devices. If you prefer, you can create your own custom download if you do not want to download the full toolkit.

Bootstrap supports styling for various widgets, including buttons and button groups, tabs, navigation bars, form controls, navigation lists, labels, and others.

Note: Bootstrap 3.0 was released just as this book went into print.

One interesting Bootstrap feature is its support for progress bars using the CSS classes `.bar` and `.progress` that are available in Bootstrap. As an illustration, the following code block shows how to render bars with different colors based on custom attributes that start with the string `progress-`, as shown here:

```
<div class="progress progress-info" style="margin-bottom: 9px;">
   <div class="bar" style="width: 20%"></div>
</div>
```

```
<div class="progress progress-success" style="margin-bottom: 9px;">
    <div class="bar" style="width: 40%"></div>
</div>
<div class="progress progress-warning" style="margin-bottom: 9px;">
    <div class="bar" style="width: 60%"></div>
</div>
<div class="progress progress-danger" style="margin-bottom: 9px;">
    <div class="bar" style="width: 80%"></div>
</div>
```

Advantages of Bootstrap

Bootstrap provides modularized components that make it a convenient starting point for Web page development. With Bootstrap you can:

- reduce design costs
- assist in creating Web pages quickly
- create dashboards easily
- adjust default values

For example, you can modify `variables.less` if you want to change the default of 12 columns, and you can change other default values (such as `@gridColumns`) to fit your needs.

Although Bootstrap contains approximately 6000 lines of CSS, you can comment out unnecessary code in `bootstrap.less` to reduce the file size.

Bootstrap also enables you to extend buttons and bars, and even provides "skins."

Disadvantages of Bootstrap

The disadvantages of Bootstrap can be different for different projects, and here are some questions that you ought to consider:

- Does Twitter Bootstrap need to work with your existing environment?
- Is Twitter Bootstrap too large for your application?
- Do you need SASS support?

You might find it necessary to override many CSS properties or edit the original CSS file (which can be problematic when a new Bootstrap version is available).

All frameworks (including Bootstrap) make assumptions that might not always be suitable for your Web pages. Some Web developers use Bootstrap as a tool for rapid Web page development in order to create a "rough draft," but not for the final product.

Semantic or Not?

Semantics is a subjective area, and differences of opinion are inevitable. Bootstrap "out of the box" does not use non-semantic markup, nor does not enforce progressive enhancement. The "non-semantic markup" means that `id` or `class` are not used semantically. Although the semantic naming of `id` or `class` was once considered a best practice, this is no longer the case after the trend of OOCSS movement.

However, a class such as `.grid_4` obviously provides no information about the content within the element, whereas a class such as `.review` or `.authorsname` makes the content more apparent. Moreover, the Bootstrap non-semantic grid system results in adding long class definitions inside HTML Web pages. For example, Bootstrap uses classes with names such as `.visible-phone`, `.visible-tablet`, and `.visible-desktop`, which might be cumbersome from a maintenance standpoint (what happens when you want to add support for mobile devices that are between phones and tablets?).

Bootstrap and H5BP (HTML5 Boilerplate)

Bootstrap and H5BP are useful for developing a prototype, but remember that Bootstrap and H5BP solve two different problems. Bootstrap is a front-end toolkit for rapid development of Web pages, whereas H5PB is more of a solid foundation. For more information, read the explanations for each section of code and markup in H5BP.

You have probably read the various aspects of the "debate" between Responsive Web Design and creating Websites that are specific to a mobile device. Regardless of your approach, make sure your code is optimized for the device. At the same time, keep in mind that Bootstrap and H5BP do not help you achieve this optimization. One possibility is to use HTML5BP, SASS/Compass, and Susy Grid for responsive design. LESS has something comparable called semantic grid system. Paul Irish has a presentation on H5BP that explains much of the "how," and has since been updated to allow for a more customized build of the H5BP download.

One interesting analogy that you might have heard is that "Bootstrap is to HTML/CSS what jQuery is to JavaScript," and there is some truth to this statement. JQuery is a powerful toolkit that is used in literally millions of Web pages. At the same time, remember that jQuery does not prevent anyone from writing inefficient code, nor does it prevent anyone from writing cross-browser and cross-platform spaghetti code.

Useful Links

A sample application using Twitter Bootstrap is here:

https://dev.twitter.com/blog/say-hello-to-bootstrap-2

Tutorials and videos:

http://webdesign.tutsplus.com/tutorials/workflow-tutorials/twitter-bootstrap-101-tabs-and-pills/

Twitter Bootstrap examples:

http://twitter.github.com/bootstrap/examples.html

An example of `Backbone.js` with Twitter Bootstrap:

http://coenraets.org/blog/2012/02/sample-app-with-backbone-js-and-twitter-bootstrap/

Various samples of Twitter snippets that you can copy/paste into your HTML5 Web pages are here:

http://bootsnipp.com/

DEBUGGING HTML5 MOBILE APPLICATIONS

Some debugging tools (such as jsconsole.com) support remote debugging on simulators as well as mobile devices. These tools offer different types of features, so you need to try them to see which ones provide the type of detail that you need for your mobile applications.

USING WEB INSPECTOR

The Web Inspector supports full JavaScript language debugging functionality. For instance, you can set breakpoints, single step through code, and display variables in your JavaScript code. In addition, you can display the HTML elements that are being rendered, examine their relationship to the display, and set breakpoints on DOM events. Moreover, you can view the effects of CSS on the DOM. Because you have access to a JavaScript console, you can view your application's console.log messages and dynamically modify your application by executing JavaScript commands.

http://webdesign.tutsplus.com/tutorials/workflow-tutorials/quick-tip-using-web-inspector-to-debug-mobile-safari/

The steps required for launching the JavaScript console depend on the browser. In Chrome:

```
View > Developer > JavaScript console
```

In Safari:

```
Develop > Show Web Inspector
```

In Internet Explorer 8 and 9:

```
Tools > Developer Tools (or use the F12 key)
```

In Opera, first find Dragonfly under:

```
Tools > Advanced (Mac OS X) or Menu > Page > Developer Tools
(Windows, Linux)
```

In Firefox 4:

```
Tools > Web Console or Menu > Web Developer > Web Console
```

Firebug added a native console that fully supports the Console API, and it has more robust CSS debugging features.

Before we discuss these tools, remember that the code samples in this book are for `WebKit`-based browsers, and in case you haven't already done so, you ought to familiarize yourself with the `Web Inspector`, which is built into Chrome and Safari. Whenever you navigate to a Web page, right-click on that Web page and you can view details about the Web page that you have launched.

For example, Figure 7.1 shows you what you will see if you launch the HTML5 Web page `HTML5Video1.html` (displayed in Listing 7.1) in a Chrome browser, right click on the page, and then click on "Resources."

The Web Inspector is a very useful tool, and it's well worth your time familiarizing yourself with its features. A Wiki page with useful information about Web Inspector is here:

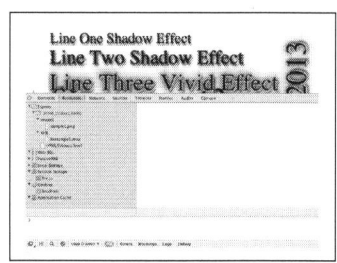

FIGURE 7.1 An Example of Chrome's Web Inspector.

http://trac.webkit.org/wiki/WebInspector
http://webdesign.tutsplus.com/tutorials/workflow-tutorials/quick-tip-using-web-inspector-to-debug-mobile-safari/
https://developers.google.com/chrome-developer-tools/docs/remote-debugging

USING PLAIN JAVASCRIPT FOR DEBUGGING

There are at least two JavaScript techniques for debugging your mobile applications. The first involves the use of a JavaScript `try/catch` block in your HTML5 Web page, and the second involves the use of `window.onerror`, both of which are supported in modern browsers.

Using JavaScript `try/catch` Blocks for Debugging

Modern browsers support the JavaScript `try/catch` block that looks like this:

```
try{
    // do something here
} catch(e) {
    console.error(e.message);
}
```

The preceding code block works in any modern browser, but this can become highly repetitive if you insert this type of error handler in multiple locations in multiple HTML5 Web pages.

Consider the second technique using "pure" JavaScript is available in modern browsers that support `window.onerror` (which includes Chrome and other WebKit-based browsers), as discussed in the next section.

Using `window.onerror` for Debugging

Unlike a `try/catch` that you saw in the previous section, you can set an event handler for `window.onerror` that captures errors you have not explicitly thrown. This scenario can happen if you try to invoke an undefined function or access an undefined variable.

The following code block illustrates a simple example of `window.on-error` in an HTML5 Web page.

```
window.onerror = errorHandler;

function errorHandler(msg,url,line) {
  var errorMsg = "Uncaught error occurred: "+msg;
  console.log(errorMsg);
  return (true);
}
```

The preceding code block is flexible, and you can customize it to accommodate your requirements. In addition, the code block appears only once in an HTML5 Web page instead of multiple `try/catch` code blocks.

USING ADOBE EDGE INSPECT

Adobe Edge Inspect (part of Adobe Creative Cloud) is a mobile debugging tool by Adobe, and its homepage is here:

http://labs.adobe.com/technologies/shadow/

Adobe Edge Inspect provides a way to test your Web sites on multiple devices simultaneously, which is also appealing if you are interested in responsive design. Adobe Edge Inspect uses WEINRE in order to perform remote DOM inspection on devices, and it currently supports Mac (OS X 10.6 and 10.7) and Windows 7. A four-minute video about Adobe Edge Inspect is here:

http://tv.adobe.com/watch/adobe-technology-sneaks-2012/adobe-shadow

Another useful debugging tool is WebKit Remote Debugging, which has been available since 2011, and it is also shipping in iOS and Android. Details are available here:

http://www.webkit.org/blog/1875/announcing-remote-debugging-protocol-v1-0/

The next portion of this chapter discusses some toolkits for debugging HTML5 Web pages.

DEBUGGING WITH `JSCONSOLE.COM`

`jsconsole` is a Web-based toolkit that enables you to perform remote debugging of hybrid HTML5 Web applications, and its homepage is here:

jsconsole.com

You can launch a Web application in a simulator, as well as iOS devices and Android devices. The home page lists the supported devices as iOS 4.2.x (iPad and iPhone 4) and Android 2.2.2 (Nexus One), but it's possible that more recent versions are supported as well (you can easily verify whether or not your device is supported).

This section shows you how to use `jsconsole` to display `console.log()` messages that are in the HTML5 Web page `ScatterAxes1.html`. Although this Web page is launched in a Chrome browser on a Macbook Pro, you can obtain the same debugging information if you embed this Web page in an HTML5 mobile application on Android or on iOS.

This Web page contains the following code snippet that will be displayed via `jsconsole` in a separate browser session:

```
console.log("Hello from ScatterAxes1.html");
```

The following set of steps describe how to start a remote debugging session in `jsconsole`, followed by section that contains a more detailed explanation of what happens when you execute the following steps.

Summary of steps

Step 1: navigate to jsconsole.com
Step 2: click on the "simply run" link (jsconsole.com/:listen)
Step 3: copy the generated <script> tag into an HTML Web page
Step 4: launch an HTML Web page containing console.log() statements

The next portion of this section provides a more detailed explanation of what happens after executing Steps #2, #3, and #4.

Detailed explanation

After Step #2 you will see the following type of information on the screen:

```
Creating connection...
Connected to "BD055707-CFBD-445A-BDB1-25BB311156B3"
<script src="http://jsconsole.com/remote.js?BD055707-CFBD-445A-
BDB1-25BB311156B3"></script>
```

After Step #3, you will see the following type of information at the bottom of the screen:

```
Connection established with file://localhost/Users/ocampesato/
aHTML5MobilePocketPrimer/manuscript/debugging-code/ScatterAxes1.
html
Mozilla/5.0 (Macintosh; Intel Mac OS X 10_8_3) AppleWebKit/537.31
(KHTML, like Gecko) Chrome/26.0.1410.65 Safari/537.31
```

After Step #4, you will also see the following type of information at the top of the screen:

```
> remote console.log
<< "Hello from ScatterAxes1.html"
```

At this point you are ready to create a remote debugging session for your own HTML5 Web pages in mobile applications.

If you want to see a live demonstration of using jsconsole, you can watch two videos here:

http://jsconsole.com/remote-debugging.html

CATALYST

Catalyst (formerly Trigger.io) is another online toolkit for testing HTML5 Web pages, and its homepage is here:

https://trigger.io/catalyst/

In order to use Catalyst, you need to embed a unique script tag into the page you wish to remotely debug. Each time this Web page is loaded in a browser session, a unique ID is generated for you (similar to `jsconsole`). Simply paste the generated `<script>` element into the top of your HTML5 Web page (the actual ID will be different):

```
<script src="https://trigger.io/catalyst/target/target-script-min.
js#EA3DA599-3A0C-44B6-AFBD-9FBB579C11BF">
</script>
```

After you have launched your modified Web page in a browser session, you can remotely view the DOM and execute JavaScript using the following link:

https://trigger.io/catalyst/client/#EA3DA599-3A0C-44B6-AFBD-9FBB579C11BF

Note: Trigger.io Catalyst is a hosted version of Weinre.

The next section shows you how to use Weinre, which is now a part of Adobe PhoneGap.

WEINRE

`WEINRE` (pronounced "winery") is an excellent debugging tool that uses the same UI display as Chrome's `Web Inspector`, and its homepage is here:

http://phonegap.github.com/weinre/

`WEINRE` supports remote debugging, which means that you can see Web pages on mobile devices. You can find YouTube videos, documentation, and discussion groups regarding `WEINRE` here:

http://www.youtube.com/results?search_query=weinre
http://callback.github.com/callback-weinre
http://groups.google.com/group/weinre
http://software.intel.com/en-us/articles/best-practices-for-debugging-cross-platform-html5-applications

If remote debugging is unavailable, you can use `Weinre` (Web Inspector Remote). `Weinre` provides a subset of the capabilities of remote debugging;

unfortunately, it does not support JavaScript debugging (such as setting break-points and single stepping through code). However, `Weinre` can access the DOM rendered in the target system and capture console output.

`Weinre` consists of three interacting components. The first component is called the debug agent. This consists of JavaScript code that must be injected into your application so it can be debugged. The second component is the `Weinre` debugger user interface that runs in the host browser. This is similar to the user interface for Chrome developer tools. The third component is the debug server, a stand-alone program used to connect the debugger user interface to your application in a secure way.

Check the `Weinre` documentation homepage for instructions on how to install and use `Weinre`, which also explains how to install and execute the debug server.

There are two ways to inject the `Weinre` debug agent into your application. You can edit your HTML5 program to add a `<script>` tag to reference the `Weinre` debug agent. If you use PhoneGap build, you can request a "debug build" from the PhoneGap Build service that automatically injects the `Weinre` debug agent into your application during packaging. PhoneGap build also provides a debug server you can use instead of running your own. See the debug build section of the PhoneGap Build documentation for more details.

Once the debug agent has been injected and the debug server is running, the last step is to connect the debugger with the program under test. The exact process used depends on which debug server you are using. See the `Weinre` documentation homepage or the debug build section of the PhoneGap Build documentation, as appropriate.

http://www.infoq.com/news/2011/07/mobile-web-debugging:
http://phonegap.com/2011/05/18/debugging-phonegap-JavaScript/

TESTING TOOLS

Several excellent performance and debugging tools are available, and this section briefly mentions several of these tools:

- Blaze (mobile Websites)
- Chrome Speed Tracer
- Page Speed Insights
- Firebug for Firefox
- Socketbug
- QUnit
- Selenium
- YUITest

In addition to the preceding tools, a good performance-related article is here:

http://cdn.oreillystatic.com/en/assets/1/event/60/Understanding%20
Mobile%20Web%20Browser%20Performance%20Presentation.pdf

Moreover, any performance-related blog posts by Steve Souders contain relevant information. You can visit his Website:

http://stevesouders.com/

Blaze

Blaze provides test results for the performance of a mobile Website, which includes overall load time as well as load times for individual pages. Blaze supports multiple mobile devices, including iPhone, iPad2 (but not iPad3), and devices with Android 2.2/2.3/3.0 (but no support yet for Android ICS).
Navigate to the following URL and follow the instructions:

http://www.blaze.io/mobile/

Chrome Speed Tracer

Chrome Speed Tracer is an open source project that assists you in identifying performance bottlenecks in your Web applications, and its homepage is here:

https://developers.google.com/web-toolkit/speedtracer/

Speed Tracer performs low-level instrumentation and after performing an analysis, the results are displayed in a visually oriented fashion. Speed Tracer is currently available as a Chrome extension and works on its supported platforms (Windows and Linux).

Page Speed Insights

PageSpeed Insights is actually a "family" of tools for optimizing the performance of Web pages, and is homepage is here:

https://developers.google.com/speed/pagespeed

The PageSpeed available tools are:

• PageSpeed browser extensions
• PageSpeed Insight
• The mod_pagespeed Apache module
• PageSpeed Service

The PageSpeed browser extensions are available for Chrome and Firefox, and help you improve the performance of your Web pages.
PageSpeed Insights is a Web-based tool that analyzes pages in any browser, without downloading an extension. The mod_pagespeed Apache module automatically rewrites pages and resources to improve their performance. Finally, PageSpeed Service is an online service that speeds up loading of your Web pages.

Firebug for Firefox

Firebug is a debugging tool that is an add-on for Firefox, and you can install Firebug here:

https://addons.mozilla.org/en-US/firefox/addon/firebug/

There are also simulation tools available, such as the one by Remy Sharp that allows you to simulate motion events on mobile devices, and its homepage is here:

http://remote-tilt.com/

You can use this tool by including one line of JavaScript in your Web pages, after which a pop-up window will appear that enables you to simulate various motion events.

Unfortunately, additional discussion about these tools is beyond the primary scope of this book, but it's definitely worth learning at least one of them, which will provide you with knowledge that you can use for debugging purposes outside of the code samples this book.

Socketbug

Socketbug is a tool created by Peter Schmalfeldt that helps you debug mobile applications, and its homepage is here:

http://socketbug.com/

SocketBug supports iOS Safari, Android Webkit, and Palm WebOS, and you can use any modern browser as your debug console.

QUnit

QUnit is the unit-testing framework that was originally built to test jQuery. It has since expanded beyond its initial goals and is now a standalone unit-testing framework. QUnit is primarily designed to be a simple solution to unit testing, providing a minimal, but easy to use, API.

Some useful and distinguishing features of QUnit include:

- Simple API
- Supports asynchronous testing
- Not limited to jQuery or jQuery-using code
- Especially well-suited for regression testing

More information can be found at *http://docs.jquery.com/Qunit*

Selenium

Selenium is a very popular browser-based utility that enables you to record and run automated tests, and its documentation page is here:

http://docs.seleniumhq.org/

YUITest

YUITest is a testing framework built and developed by Yahoo! and released in October of 2008. It was completely rewritten in 2009 to coincide with the release of YUI 3. YUITest provides an impressive number of features and functionality that is sure to cover any unit testing case required by your code base.

Distinguishing features include:

- Extensive and comprehensive unit testing functionality
- Supports asynchronous tests
- Good event simulation

More information is available at *http://developer.yahoo.com/yui/3/test/*

JAVASCRIPT TESTING TOOLS FOR HTML5 MOBILE APPS

There are various JavaScript testing tools available, and this section briefly mentions two of these testing tools.

The first testing tool is JSUnit, which is a port of the popular Java JUnit testing framework to JavaScript, and its homepage is here:

http://www.jsunit.net/

While it's still one of the most popular JavaScript unit testing frameworks around, JSUnit is also one of the oldest (both in terms of the code base age and quality). The framework hasn't been updated much recently, so for something that's known to work with all modern browsers, JSUnit may not be the best choice.

Another testing tool is JSBin, which is a pre-built service designed for creating simple test cases, and its homepage is here:

http://jsbin.com/

Each test case becomes available at a unique URL, and you can even include copies of some of the most popular JavaScript libraries.

Perform an Internet search to obtain more information about these and other JavaScript testing tools for HTML5 Mobile applications.

CODE VALIDATORS: JSLINT AND JSHINT

JSLint.com allows you to cut and paste your code into a form and it will validate your code, and its homepage is here:

http://www.jslint.com/lint.html

Douglas Crockford is the author of JSLint, which checks for syntax errors, style conventions, and structural problems based on a subset of the Third Edition of the ECMAScript Programming Language Standard.

An explanation of many (but not all) JSLint errors is here:

http://jslinterrors.com/

JSHint.com is a useful alternative if you feel that JSLint.com is too restrictive, and its homepage is here:

http://www.jshint.com/

Navigate to the preceding link and copy/paste your code in the text area, and then click the "Lint" button to see the analysis of your code.

Note that you can also install JSHint as a NodeJS module.

TOOLS FOR REDUCING REFLOW AND REPAINT IN WEB PAGES

Before discussing techniques for finding performance-related issues in Web pages, some terminology is required. In Gekko, *reflow* refers to the process of calculating the position of elements in a Web page, and *repaint* refers to the re-rendering of pixel colors in a Web page, whereas Chrome uses the term *layout* instead of *reflow*.

Many common events (as well as CSS3 features) cause reflows and repaints, including:

- scroll and hover
- modifying the DOM in any fashion
- opacity
- border radius (more expensive than gradients)
- linear and radial gradients
- drop shadows
- transitions

When there are too many reflows and repaints, an entire Web page can become sluggish. The next section describes how to use an option in Chrome Canary that can help you detect performance-related issues in CSS selectors.

Enabling Continuous Painting Mode

Chrome Canary provides a "continuous painting mode" option that helps you find bottlenecks in painting performance. Enable continuous painting mode as follows:

1. Open the Web Inspector.
2. Click on the cog in the lower-right corner of the screen.
3. Click on the checkbox "Enable continuous page repainting"

The display in the top-right corner of the screen provides the following measurements (in milliseconds) pertaining to paint times:

- The last measured paint time (on the left)
- The minimum and maximum of the current graph (on the right)
- A bar chart with the history of the last 80 frames on the bottom

In addition, the line in the bar chart indicates 16 ms as a reference point. Now that you know how to enable continuous painting mode, the next section describes a process for finding performance bottlenecks.

Finding CSS-Related Performance Bottlenecks

Enable continuous painting mode in Chrome Canary as described previously and generate a Timeline containing performance statistics as follows:

1. Navigate to the Elements panel and traverse the DOM tree with the arrow keys (or by selecting elements on the page)
2. Use the H keyboard shortcut in order to toggle visibility on an element
3. Inspect the paint time graph and search for elements that significantly increase the painting time
4. Navigate to the CSS styles of that element and watch the graph as you toggle them on and off (one at a time) to determine which style causes a performance lag
5. Modify the style in the preceding step and now generate another Timeline recording to verify whether or not this modification has improved the performance of your Web page

The preceding set of steps provide you with an iterative process by which you can pinpoint which combination of CSS styles and DOM elements are contributing to a performance degradation.

ADDITIONAL USEFUL LINKS

A more recent Website is `HTML5 Please`, which consists of contributions from well-known industry people:

http://html5please.com

The preceding Website provides an input field where you can specify HTML5 and CSS3 features to determine if they are ready for use, and also see how to use them.

The W3C provides a free online validation service for HTML Web pages, including HTML5 Web pages:

http://validator.w3.org/#validate_by_uri+with_options

The preceding Website enables you to validate of a URL, a file, or direct input of code.

The following Website provides "boilerplate" templates for HTML5 e-mail input fields (and also templates for CSS and jQuery):

http://favbulous.com/post/848/6-useful-web-development-boilerplates

The following two links are for the HTML5 draft specification and the HTML5 draft recommendation (May, 2009)

http://www.w3.org/TR/html5/
http://www.whatwg.org/specs/web-apps/current-work/

There is also a "Web developer edition" of the HTML5 specification that is streamlined for readability (without vendor-oriented details) that you can read here:

http://developers.whatwg.org

IMPROVING HTML5 WEB PAGE PERFORMANCE

Performance is always an important consideration, and although a detailed and lengthy discussion is beyond the constraints of this book, it's important to be aware of some of the techniques that are available:

- concatenate JavaScript/CSS files into a single file
- use file compression (minification)
- use of spritesheets
- use base64 encoding of images
- defer the loading of JavaScript files

A good blog post regarding the use of base64 for encoding images is here:

http://davidbcalhoun.com/2011/when-to-base64-encode-images-and-when-not-to?goback=%2Egde_2071438_member_234328886

You can defer the loading of JavaScript files by placing `<script>` tags at the end of the `<body>` element in a Web page.

You can also explore `RequireJS`, which is a JavaScript toolkit for asynchronously downloading JavaScript files (as well as managing JavaScript dependencies), and its homepage is here:

http://requirejs.org/

Steve Souders has written at least two performance-related books and has written many blog posts regarding performance, and it's definitely worth reading his work.

CSS-RELATED PERFORMANCE

CSS3 provides wonderful functionality, such as rounded corners, as well as 2D and 3D graphics and animation effects. However, CSS3 features can differ in terms of performance, which obviously affects the performance of an HTML5 Web page.

Recall that you can guarantee that the GPU will be used on a device by using something such as `translate3D(0,0,0)`, which is essentially a "no operation." You can also replace 2D transforms by their corresponding 3D transforms. However, an indiscriminate use of 3D transforms can cause a page reflow or a page repaint, which has an adverse impact on performance.

Good articles regarding CSS paint times are here:

- *http://css-tricks.com/efficiently-rendering-css/*

- *http://www.html5rocks.com/en/tutorials/speed/css-paint-times/*
- *http://stickmanventures.com/labs/demo/spinning-gears-Chrome-preserve-3d/#*

Another interesting point pertains to the use of CSS3 translate versus absolute position in a CSS selector. Paul Irish compares these techniques here:

http://paulirish.com/2012/why-moving-elements-with-translate-is-better-than-posabs-topleft/

If you are interested in the lower-level details about the painting process, CSS2 defines the order of the painting process, which is the order in which the elements are stacked in the "stacking contexts." This order affects painting because the stacks are painted from back to front. The stacking order of a block renderer is here:

1. background color
2. background image
3. border
4. children
5. outline

A more detailed explanation of the painting process is here:

http://www.html5rocks.com/en/tutorials/speed/unnecessary-paints/
http://www.html5rocks.com/en/tutorials/internals/howbrowserswork/

USEFUL LINKS

The following links are helpful for testing Mobile applications:

- *http://css3test.com/*
- *http://www.css3.info/selectors-test/*
- *http://quirksmode.org/html5/tests/video.html*
- *http://double.co.nz/video_test/*
- *http://www.terrillthompson.com/tests/html5-audio.html*

Other resources include www.stackoverflow.com and videos by Paul Irish.

SUMMARY

This chapter showed you several design strategies for HTML5 Web pages and hybrid HTML5 mobile applications. Next, you learned about toolkits for debugging your mobile Web pages. You also learned about techniques for testing mobile Web pages. Finally, you learned about performance-related considerations for hybrid HTML5 mobile applications.

CHAPTER 8

INTRODUCTION TO JQUERY MOBILE

This chapter contains an introduction to jQuery Mobile that shows you how to create HTML5-based applications using jQuery Mobile. Web pages for desktop browsers are rendered differently on mobile devices, which is immediately apparent whenever you see the tiny font size of the rendered text on a mobile device. Fortunately, jQuery Mobile is highly "page aware" and it provides many useful before-and-after page-related events that you can override with customizations that are tailored to your needs.

In fact, jQuery Mobile is designed around the notion of (mostly) single-page applications with multiple "page views" (discussed later in this chapter), whereas jQuery was designed when multi-page sites and applications were predominant. Thus, jQuery Mobile has a view-oriented model, whereas jQuery has a Web page-oriented model. This important distinction will help you understand the rationale for the features that are available in jQuery Mobile.

In this chapter, you will become well-acquainted with the `data-` prefix in custom attributes, which are part of the HTML5 specification (Section 3.2.3.8). JQuery Mobile makes extensive use of custom attributes with a `data-` prefix, whereas custom attributes are not used in jQuery. In fact, jQuery Mobile uses this custom attribute for specifying behavior, functionality, and layout. As you will see, two frequently used custom attributes are `data-role` and `data-transition`.

If you want to write Web pages that display correctly on different devices, then at a minimum, you need to take into account the dimensions (width and height) of those devices. Other considerations include (but are not limited to) DPI (dots per inch), which varies between mobile devices, and whether or not you want to allow users to pinch or zoom into the Web page. One of the strengths of jQuery Mobile is that device differences are handled automatically for you, in addition to its rich feature set and its support for many mobile platforms.

The first part of this chapter provides an overview of some features of jQuery Mobile, as well as some important differences from jQuery. You will see how jQuery Mobile programmatically enhances your Web pages with extra functionality that reduces the coding effort on your part in order to create mobile-enabled Web pages, and also ensures that your Web pages will render correctly on different mobile devices. In addition, you will learn about page-related events that are exposed by jQuery Mobile (there are many of them), and some of the default behavior that you can override programmatically.

The second part of this chapter discusses multi-page views in jQuery Mobile, and various ways for positioning headers and footers. The third part of this chapter discusses buttons in jQuery Mobile, which is an extensive topic with lots of rich functionality, and you will see complete code samples and useful code snippets.

The fourth part of this chapter contains code samples that illustrate how to work with various widgets, including list views, navigation bars, and menus in jQuery Mobile. The intent of these code samples is to show you not just how to use these widgets, but also how to incorporate CSS3-based graphics effects in the code samples. Some of these effects, such as shadow and gradients (which you learned how to do in Chapter 3), show you how to create a richer visual effect that goes beyond the "out of the box" functionality of jQuery Mobile. The final portion of this chapter contains code samples that show you how to use Ajax and Geolocation in HTML Web pages with jQuery Mobile.

USING JQUERY 2.0

The following code samples work correctly in jQuery2.0.0, but they report "spurious" warnings that you can see when you launch them in a WebKit-based browser and then open the Web Inspector:

- `JQMAjax1.html`
- `JQMButtons1.html`
- `JQMFixed1.html`
- `JQMForm1.html`
- `JQMHelloWorld1.html`
- `JQMMenu1.html`
- `JQMNavigationBar1.html`
- `JQMNestedListViews1.html`
- `JQMPageEvents1.html`
- `JQMSimpleListView1.html`
- `JQMMultiPageViews1.html`
- `JQMGeolocation1.html`

OVERVIEW OF JQUERY MOBILE

jQuery Mobile is essentially a collection of jQuery plug-ins and widgets that enable you to write mobile Web applications that run on multiple platforms. You already know that jQuery focuses on desktop Web applications; by contrast, jQuery Mobile (which includes a CSS stylesheet and a JavaScript library) is intended for mobile devices. However, jQuery Mobile does rely on the "base" jQuery library that you must reference prior to referencing the jQuery Mobile library in a Web page. In addition, jQuery Mobile uses features of HTML5 and CSS3 (such as transitions and animation), and small icons for navigation.

jQuery Mobile relies on custom attributes with a `data-` prefix. In case you do not know, custom attributes are new in HTML5, and they always have such a prefix. This support for custom data attributes provides HTML5 markup with some of the functionality that is available in XML, which enables code to process custom tags and their values and also pass validation at the same time.

A simple jQuery Mobile page has the following structure:

- an optional `<div>` element with a `data-role="header"` attribute
- a mandatory `<div>` element with a `data-role="content"` attribute
- an optional `<div>` element with a `data-role="footer"` attribute

During initialization, jQuery Mobile pre-processes a Web page and inserts additional markup, CSS classes, and event handlers. You will see an example of how jQuery Mobile modifies a Web page in the "Hello World" code sample later in this chapter.

There are several important details that you need to be aware of when writing jQuery Mobile Web pages. First, jQuery Mobile provides the following page-related events that you can invoke programmatically during the lifecycle of a jQuery Mobile page: `pageInit()`, `pageCreate()`, `pageShow()`, and `pageHide()`. Second, jQuery Mobile supports custom events for handling user gestures such as `swipe`, `tap`, `tap-and-hold`, and `orientation` changes of a device. Third, jQuery Mobile uses themes to customize the look-and-feel of mobile applications, along with progressive enhancement (discussed briefly in Chapter 1) to enable your mobile application to run on a diverse set of Web-enabled devices.

Another key point to keep in mind is that jQuery uses this construct:

```
$(document).ready() {
  // do something here
}
```

On the other hand, jQuery Mobile uses this construct:

```
$(selector).live('pageinit', (function(event){
  // do something here
}));
```

Notice the different focus: JQuery sends an event when a Web page has been loaded, whereas jQuery Mobile sends an event when a page (or page view) has been initialized.

Key Features and Components in jQuery Mobile

If you have read the previous chapters that cover jQuery, you have already acquired substantial knowledge of jQuery features. This knowledge is useful for another reason: jQuery Mobile uses jQuery as its foundation, and the jQuery library must always precede the jQuery Mobile library in your HTML5 Web pages.

jQuery Mobile provides many useful features that will simplify the process of creating mobile applications. Some of the jQuery Mobile features are listed here:

- compatible with major mobile platforms (Android, iOS, and others)
- uses HTML5 markup
- adopts progressive enhancement approach
- provides a compact toolkit (about 12K compressed)
- supports plugins and themes
- supports touch and mouse-based user gestures
- supports WAI-ARIA

In addition, jQuery Mobile supports the following components (and others that are not listed here):

- Buttons
- Form elements
- List views
- Pages and dialogs
- Toolbars

The jQuery code samples in this book use a simple naming convention: the names of HTML5 Web pages that contain jQuery code start with "JQ," and the names of HTML5 Web pages that contain jQuery Mobile start with the letters "JQM." Keep in mind that this naming convention is only for this book.

A MINIMAL JQUERY MOBILE WEB PAGE

Listing 8.1 displays the contents of JQMHelloWorld1.html that illustrates how to display the message "Hello World" in an HTML5 Web page that is rendered on a desktop browser, tablet, or smart phone.

LISTING 8.1: JQMHelloWorld1.html

```
<!DOCTYPE html>
<html lang="en">
  <head>
   <meta charset=utf-8" />
   <title>Hello World from jQuery Mobile</title>
```

```
<link rel="stylesheet"
  href="http://code.jquery.com/mobile/1.1.0/jquery.mobile-
1.1.0.min.css" />
  <script src="http://code.jquery.com/jquery-2.0.0b1.js">
  </script>
  <script src="http://code.jquery.com/jquery-migrate-1.1.0.js">
  </script>

  <script
  src="http://code.jquery.com/mobile/1.1.0/jquery.mobile-1.1.0.min.js">
  </script>
  </head>

  <body>
    <div  data-role="page">
      <div data-role="header">
        <h2>This is the Header</h2>
      </div>
      <div data-role="content">
        <p>Hello World from a Simple jQuery Mobile Page</p>
      </div>
      <div data-role="footer">
        <h2>This is the Footer</h2>
      </div>
    </div>
  </body>
</html>
```

Listing 8.1 is straightforward: it consists of a single page view (an HTML `<div>` element with a `data-role="page"` attribute) that contains three `<div>` elements: a header section, the content section, and the footer section, respectively.

Figure 8.1 displays the result of rendering the HTML Web page in Listing 8.1 in a landscape-mode screenshot taken from an Asus Prime tablet with Android ICS.

Compare Figure 8.1 with Figure 8.2, which shows the sample jQuery Mobile application running on a Sprint Nexus S 4G smart phone with Android ICS in landscape mode, using the same Android apk binary that was used for capturing Figure 8.1. Notice how the header and footer extend automatically to the width of the screen in both screenshots.

Now launch Listing 8.1 in a `Webkit`-based browser, and compare what you see in Figure 8.1 and Figure 8.2.

FIGURE 8.1 "Hello World" on an Asus Prime Tablet with Android ICS (landscape mode).

FIGURE 8.2 "Hello World" on a Sprint Nexus S 4G with Android ICS (landscape mode).

Earlier you learned that jQuery Mobile enhances a mobile Web page with additional tags and CSS classes. jQuery Mobile "injects" various CSS classes (that are part of jQuery Mobile) into the HTML5 Web page in Listing 8.1. In general, you will not need to be concerned with these details; however, you can delve into the jQuery Mobile source code if you need a deeper understanding of these details. The HTML5 page `JQMHelloWorld1Enhanced.html` on the DVD shows you how jQuery "enhances" the contents of the HTML5 Web page `HelloWorld1.html`.

MORE DIFFERENCES BETWEEN JQUERY AND JQUERY MOBILE

jQuery is a toolkit for creating HTML Web pages on desktop browser, whereas jQuery Mobile provides support for additional functionality that is relevant for mobile devices:

- support for multiple page views
- custom attributes with a `data-` prefix for page views and transitions
- page transitions (`pagebeforehide`, `pagebeforeshow`, and so forth)
- the `jqmData()` custom selector
- the `mobileInit` event

jQuery Mobile Page Views

As you saw in a previous code sample, each page view in a jQuery Mobile application is defined by an HTML `<div>` element with a `data-role="page"` attribute, along with an optional header element, a mandatory content element, and an optional footer element.

Navigation between page views is straightforward: simply add a link to the `<div>` element with the `data-role="content"` attribute in the jQuery Mobile application, as shown here:

```
<div data-role="content">
  <p>A second page view<a href="#home">Home</a></p>
</div>
```

The transition between page views occurs when users tap on a link, and jQuery Mobile automatically handles the necessary details of the transition. A complete example of a jQuery Mobile Web page with multiple page views (and how to navigate between the page views) is provided later in this chapter.

jQuery Mobile Custom Attributes

JQuery Mobile uses the `data-role` attribute to identify different parts of a "page view" (which is essentially one screen), and some of its supported values are `page`, `header`, `content`, and `footer`. The `data-role` attribute is also used to enhance HTML elements. For example, if you specify the attribute `data-role="listview"` as part of the HTML `<ul>` tag of an unordered list, then jQuery Mobile will make the necessary enhancements (such as inserting markup, adding CSS classes, and exposing listeners) so that you can treat the unordered list as though it were a widget.

As another example, you can create a navigation bar by adding the attribute `data-role="navbar"` to the block-level HTML5 `<nav>` element, and the text strings in the associated list items (which are enclosed in the HTML5 `<nav>` element) are displayed as tab elements in the navigation bar.

The `data-transition` attribute specifies transition effects when changing page views or when displaying dialogs. Because these transitions are based on CSS3, these transitions work only in browsers that support CSS3 (such as WebKit-based browsers). The allowable values for the `data-transition` attribute are `fade`, `flip`, `pop`, `slide`, `slidedown`, and `slideup`.

Some of the other custom jQuery Mobile attributes are `data-backbtn`, `data-divider`, `data-direction`, `data-icon`, `data-inline`, `data-position`, `data-rel`, and `data-url`.

jQuery Mobile Page Transitions

jQuery Mobile provides page transitions, as well as the `event` and `ui` objects, that you can reference in custom code blocks that you bind to any page transition. Keep in mind that a "page" can be a separate HTML Web page as well as an HTML `<div>` element inside the currently loaded HTML Web page.

Here is the sequence of page events that occurs during a page initialization:

```
pagebeforecreate: fires first
pagecreate: fires when DOM is populated
pageinit: after initialization is completed
pagebeforeshow: fires on 'to' page before transition
pageshow: fires on 'to' page after transition
```

Whenever users tap a link that navigates to a page that is loaded for the first time, the following sequence of events occurs:

```
pagebeforehide: fires on the 'from' page before transition
pagebeforeshow: fires on the 'to' page before transition
pagehide: fires on the 'from' page after transition
pageshow: fires on the 'to' page after transition
```

Whenever a new page is loaded using Ajax, the following sequence of events occurs:

```
pagebeforeload: before the AJAX call is made
pageload: after the AJAX call is completed
pageloadfailed: fired if an AJAX call has failed
```

During page transitions, `ui.nextPage` is assigned the target page of the transition, or an empty jQuery object if there is no next page. Similarly, `ui.prevPage` is assigned the current page prior to the transition, or an empty jQuery object if there is no previous page.

jQuery Mobile uses Ajax-based asynchronous method invocations for its internal functionality, so it distinguishes page load events from page show and hide events. Page load events occur when a file is loaded into the browser in a synchronous manner, and the jQuery(document).ready() method is available, along with other initialization events. Note that in some cases you can explicitly specify synchronous instead of asynchronous method invocation, but this feature is not discussed in this chapter (check the online jQuery Mobile documentation if you want more details).

As you will see later in this chapter, a single HTML Web page may contain multiple jQuery Mobile page views, and users can navigate among those page views multiple times. These transitions do not fire page load events; jQuery Mobile provides a set of events that happen every time a page transition occurs.

Because the page hide and show events are triggered every time a page transition happens, make sure that you do not bind the event handlers more than once by first checking if the event handler is not already bound (otherwise do nothing), or by clearing the binding prior to rebinding to a given event.

Listing 8.2 displays the contents of JQMPageEvents1.html that illustrates the sequence in which page events are executed.

LISTING 8.2: JQMPageEvents1.html

```
<!DOCTYPE html>
<html lang="en">
<head>
 <meta charset="utf-8">
 <title>JQuery Mobile Page Events`</title>

 <link rel="stylesheet"
  href="http://code.jquery.com/mobile/1.1.0/jquery.mobile-1.1.0.min.
css" />

  <script src="http://code.jquery.com/jquery-2.0.0b1.js">
  </script>
  <script src="http://code.jquery.com/jquery-migrate-1.1.0.js">
  </script>

  <script src="http://code.jquery.com/mobile/1.1.0/jquery.mobile-
1.1.0.min.js"> </script>
 </head>

 <body>
  <div data-role="page" id="page1">
    <div data-role="header">
      <h3>JQuery Mobile Page Events</h3>
    </div>
    <div data-role="content" id="content">
    </div>
    <div data-role="footer"><h3>Footer</h3></div>
  </div>

  <script>
    $("#page1").live('pagebeforecreate', (function(event){
       console.log("pagebeforecreate event");
      })
    );
```

```
$("#page1").live('pagecreate', (function(event){
    console.log("pagecreate event");
  })
);

$("#page1").live('pageinit', (function(event){
    console.log("pageinit event");
  })
);

$("#page1").live('pagebeforehide', (function(event){
    console.log("pagebeforehideevent");
  })
);

$("#page1").live('pagebeforeshow', (function(event){
    console.log("pagebeforeshow event");
  })
);

$("#page1").live('pagehide', (function(event){
    console.log("pagehide event");
  })
);

$("#page1").live('pageshow', (function(event){
    console.log("pageshow event");
  })
);
</script>
</body>
</html>
```

Listing 8.2 is a simple HTML5 Web page with HTML markup and jQuery Mobile code for a single page view. The main block of code uses the jQuery `live()` method to bind various page-related events, which displays a message in the console whenever the page event occurs.

Figure 8.3 displays the result of rendering the HTML Web page in Listing 8.2 in a Chrome browser on a Macbook. The Chrome Inspector at the bottom of Figure 8.3 shows you the sequence of paged-related events that are fired in jQuery Mobile.

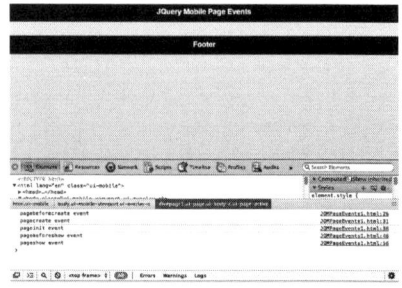

FIGURE 8.3 jQuery Mobile Page Events on a Chrome Browser on a Macbook.

jQuery Mobile and CSS-related Page Initialization

In addition to exposing page-related events, jQuery Mobile performs additional processing on an HTML Web page before the Web page is rendered in a browser. First, jQuery Mobile triggers the `beforecreate` event and then adds the `ui-page` class to all page elements, and also adds the `ui-nojs` class to all page elements which have `data-role="none"` or `data-role="nojs"` applied to them.

Next, jQuery Mobile searches for child elements with a `data-` attribute and adds theming classes, an appropriate ARIA role, and (if necessary) also adds a back button to the header for any pages beyond the first page.

Finally, jQuery Mobile enhances buttons, control groups, and form controls, and makes any necessary adjustments to toolbars.

Thus, jQuery Mobile performs a significant amount of work on your behalf, which means that you are unencumbered with these tedious and low-level details so that you can concentrate on the functionality of your mobile applications.

There is even more good news: jQuery Mobile automatically handles page transitions and back buttons as users navigate through the various pages of your mobile application, and also handle external pages by performing an asynchronous fetch (using Ajax) and then integrating that external page into the current document (and an error message is displayed if the external page was not found). The external page is incorporated into the first element with a `data-role="page"` attribute into the current document (and all other content of that page is ignored).

Note that jQuery Mobile displays an error message if it cannot find the Web page or if the Web page does not contains an element with a `data-role="page"` attribute. Make sure that the `id` values in the external Web page are distinct from the `id` values of the current Web page.

By the way, you can override the default page loading in two ways: specifying a target attribute on a link (such as `_blank`) or by specifying a `rel="external"` attribute on the link.

The `mobileinit` Event

jQuery Mobile triggers the `mobileinit` event on the document object immediately upon execution, so you can bind to it and override any default configuration.

For instance, suppose you need to prevent jQuery Mobile from applying styling rules to specific types of HTML elements throughout a mobile application. The following code block prevents jQuery Mobile from applying its styling rules (on a global level) to HTML `<input>` and `<textarea>` elements:

```
$(document).bind('mobileinit',function () {
    $.mobile.page.prototype.options.keepNative = "input, textarea";
});
```

Note that the `data-role="none"` attribute serves the same purpose as the previous code block, except that it is only applied to the specific element that includes this attribute.

JQUERY MOBILE OPTIONS AND CUSTOMIZATION

jQuery Mobile provides options and methods for various objects, including .mobile, .mobile.path, and .mobile.history. There are many options that you can configure for your mobile application, and we'll cover just a few of them in this section. One method that is obviously useful is the jQuery Mobile pageLoading() method that shows and hides the jQuery Mobile loading dialog. You call this method with a Boolean value of true to hide the dialog, and call this method without a parameter to show the dialog, as shown here:

```
// Show the page loading dialog
$.mobile.pageLoading();

// Hide the loading dialog
$.mobile.pageLoading(true);
```

You can also customize the "loading message" and also the type of transition effect, as shown here:

```
$.mobile.loadingMessage = "wait a few moments ";
$.mobile.defaultPageTransition = "pop";
```

Another way of doing the same thing as the previous two lines is shown here:

```
$.extent($.mobile, {
    "loadingMessage" = "wait a few moments",
    "defaultPageTransition" = "pop"
});
```

In fact, you can configure jQuery Mobile with your own initialization as follows: 1) create a script that loads before jQuery Mobile is loaded, and 2) bind an event handler to the mobileinit event.

If you want more information about jQuery Mobile custom initialization, options, and methods, read the jQuery documentation for an in-depth explanation of how you can use them.

PAGE NAVIGATION AND CHANGING PAGES

As users navigate around your mobile Web application, jQuery Mobile also updates the location.hash object, with the unique URL of each page view (which is defined by an element with a data-role="page" attribute). jQuery Mobile automatically stores the URL for each page is stored in the data-url attribute which jQuery Mobile assigns to the "container" element of a page.

jQuery Mobile also provides a set of methods that enable you to programmatically handle page changes and scrolling. One of these methods is changePage(), whose syntax looks like this:

```
changePage(to, transition, back, changeHash);
```

The `to` parameter is a string that specifies an element ID or a filename (along with many other options), and it is a reference to the target page. The `transition` parameter is the name of the transition effect that is created when the application goes to the target page. The `back` parameter is a Boolean value that specifies whether or not a transition is in reverse. Finally, the `changeHash` parameter is a Boolean that specifies whether or not to update the `location.hash` object.

The `changePage()` method enables you to create more sophisticated page transition effects. For example, the following code snippet goes to page `#first` when users click on the `.back-btn`, with a "flip" effect in reverse without updating the location hash:

```
$(".back-btn").bind("click", function() {
  changePage("#first", "flip", true, false);
});
```

jQuery Mobile also provides the `silentScroll()` method with a single integer value that specifies the y-position of the destination. When this method is invoked, the scroll event listeners are not triggered. As an example, the following code snippet scrolls down to position 200:

```
$.mobile.silentScroll(200);
```

The `jqmData()` Custom Selector

In Chapter 1, you learned about the jQuery `data()` method, and jQuery Mobile provides a corresponding method called `jqmData()`, which is a custom selector specifically for selecting custom `data-` attributes.

For example, in jQuery you can select all the elements in a Web page that contain a `data-role` attribute whose value is `page` using this code snippet:

```
$("[data-role='page']")
```

You can select the same set of elements using `jqmData()` as shown here:

```
$(":jqmData(role='page')")
```

Select all elements with any custom `data-` attribute within those selected pages:

```
$(":jqmData(role='page')").jqmData(role)
```

Note that the `jqmData()` selector automatically handles namespacing for you by specifying a value for the string `namespace-` (which is empty by default), thereby avoiding tagname collisions.

MULTIPLE PAGE VIEWS IN ONE HTML5 WEB PAGE

jQuery Mobile enables you to conveniently define multiple page views in a single HTML5 Web page, along with a simple mechanism for users to navigate among the different page views in the HTML5 Web page. The use of a single HTML5 Web page is recommended because this approach is more efficient than creating a mobile application with multiple HTML5 Web pages. Although the initial download for the HTML5 Web page might be longer, there are no additional Internet accesses required when users navigate to different parts of the Web page.

Listing 8.3 displays the contents of JQMMultiPageViews1.html that illustrates how to navigate between multiple internal page views in a single HTML5 Web page.

LISTING 8.3: JQMMultiPageViews1.html

```
<!DOCTYPE html>
<html>
<head>
  <meta charset=utf-8" />
  <title>jQuery Mobile: Multiple Page Views</title>

  <link rel="stylesheet"
    href="http://code.jquery.com/mobile/1.1.0/jquery.mobile-
1.1.0.min.css" />

  <script src="http://code.jquery.com/jquery-2.0.0b1.js">
  </script>
  <script src="http://code.jquery.com/jquery-migrate-1.1.0.js">
  </script>

  <script src="http://code.jquery.com/mobile/1.1.0/jquery.mobile-
1.1.0.min.js">
  </script>
</head>

 <body>
  <div data-role="page" id="home">
    <div data-role="header"> <h1>Home Page Header</h1> </div>
    <div data-role="content">
      <p>This is the content of the main page</p>
      <p><a href="#about">Click here to get more information</a></p>
    </div>
    <div data-role="footer"> <h1>Home Page Footer</h1> </div>
  </div>

  <div data-role="page" id="about">
    <div data-role="header"> <h1>About This Page Header</h1> </div>
    <div data-role="content">
      <p>A second page view (that's all for now)</p>
      <a href="#home"> Click Here or the 'Back' Button to go Home</a>
    </div>
    <div data-role="footer"> <h1>About This Page Footer</h1> </div>
  </div>
 </body>
</html>
```

Listing 8.3 contains two page views, as specified by the HTML `<div>` elements whose `id` attribute has value `home` and `about` (shown in bold in Listing 8.3). When users navigate to the second page view, this code snippet returns to the first page view:

```
<a href="#home"> Click Here or the 'Back' Button to go Home</a>
```

The page views or screens in a jQuery Mobile application are top-level sibling elements, each of which contains the attribute `data-role="page"` (so pages cannot be nested).

The jQuery Mobile framework automatically generates a back button and a home button on every page view, but you can suppress the back button by specifying the `data-backbtn="false"` attribute, as shown here:

```
<div data-role="header" data-backbtn="false">
  <h1>Page Header</h1>
</div>
```

Figure 8.4 displays the result of rendering the HTML Web page in Listing 8.3 in a landscape-mode screenshot taken from a Sprint Nexus S 4G with Android ICS.

When you click on the link on the Web page, the application navigates to the second screen, whose code definition is also included in Listing 8.3.

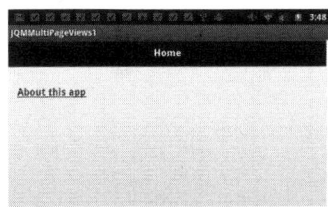

FIGURE 8.4 Multi-Page App on a Sprint Nexus S 4G with Android ICS.

POSITIONING THE HEADER AND FOOTER IN PAGE VIEWS

jQuery Mobile can dynamically position the header and footer toolbars in three ways:

1. **Standard**: The toolbars are presented according to the document flow, scrolling into and out of the viewport as the user scrolls through data. This is the default.
2. **Fixed**: The header and footer will appear at the top and bottom of the viewport and remain there as the user scrolls. Tapping on the screen will cause them to return to their regular position in the document flow.
3. **Fullscreen**: The header and footer will appear within the viewport and stay present as the user scrolls, regardless of where the user is in the content. Tapping on the screen will hide them. Essentially, the header and footer are removed from the document flow and are always dynamically positioned at the top and bottom of the viewport.

Include the `data-position="fixed"` attribute in the `<header>` or `<footer>` tags to create a fixed header and footer, as illustrated in Listing 8.4 that displays the contents of `JQMFixed1.html`.

LISTING 8.4: JQMFixed1.html

```html
<!DOCTYPE html>
<html lang="en">
 <head>
   <meta charset="utf-8" />
   <title>Fixed Header and Footer in jQueryMobile</title>

   <link rel="stylesheet"
   href="http://code.jquery.com/mobile/1.1.0/jquery.mobile-
1.1.0.min.css" />
   <script src="http://code.jquery.com/jquery-2.0.0b1.js">
   </script>
   <script src="http://code.jquery.com/jquery-migrate-1.1.0.js">
   </script>

   <script
src="http://code.jquery.com/mobile/1.1.0/jquery.mobile-1.1.0.min.js">
   </script>
 </head>

 <body>
   <div id="page1" data-role="page">
     <header data-role="header" data-position="fixed">
       <h1>jQuery Mobile</h1>
     </header>
     <div class="content" data-role="content">
       <h3>Content area.</h3>
     </div>
     <footer data-role="footer" data-position="fixed">
       <h3>Fixed Footer</h3>
     </footer>
   </div>
 </body>
</html>
```

Listing 8.4 contains HTML markup and a single page view that also specifies the attribute `data-position="fixed"` for the header and footer elements.

You can also create a fullscreen header or a fullscreen footer by including the attribute `data-fullscreen="true"` in the element that contains the `data-role="page"` attribute, along with the attribute `data-position="fixed"` to the header and footer elements, as shown here:

```html
<section id="page1" data-role="page" data-fullscreen="true">
  <header data-role="header" data-position="fixed">
    <h1>jQuery Mobile</h1>
  </header>
  <div class="content" data-role="content">
    <h3>Content area</h3>
  </div>
  <footer data-role="footer" data-position="fixed">
    <h3>Mercury Learning</h3> </footer>
  </div>
</section>
<p><a href="#about" data-transition="flip">About this app</a></p>
```

Figure 8.5 displays the result of rendering the HTML5 Web page in Listing 8.4 in a Chrome browser on a Macbook.

Launch the HTML5 Web page in Listing 8.5 in a Chrome browser, and as you resize your browser horizontally or vertically, notice how the header and footer "bar" remain anchored to the top and the bottom of the screen, respectively.

FIGURE 8.5 Fixed Headers/Footers in a Chrome browser on a Macbook.

Now that you understand the structure of an HTML5 Web page in jQuery Mobile, let's see how to add jQuery Mobile buttons to an HTML5 Web page.

WORKING WITH BUTTONS IN JQUERY MOBILE

JQuery Mobile provides a set of button markup options that enable you to style links as buttons, and also built-in support for automatically handling various types of HTML `<input>` elements as though they were buttons. In addition, JQuery Mobile supports inline buttons, grouped buttons (both vertical and horizontal), and an assortment of theming effects for buttons.

JQuery Mobile creates stylized buttons by applying `data-role="button"` to HTML `<input>` buttons, `<button>` tags, and anchor links. Buttons are as wide as their containing element; however, if you specify the attribute `data-inline="true"`, then buttons are rendered only as wide as their content.

In some of the earlier versions (prior to 1.7) of jQuery Mobile, you could prevent jQuery Mobile from applying its styling to a button by placing your custom markup inside an HTML `<div>` element that is located inside the HTML5 `<header>` element. However, this functionality is no longer available in version 1.7 (and beyond), so keep this in mind in case you encounter this functionality in Web pages that use older versions of jQuery Mobile.

You can also create a reverse transition without going back in history by using the attribute `data-direction="reverse"` instead of `data-rel="back"`, as shown here:

```
<div data-role="header">
  <a href="index.html" data-direction="reverse">Reverse Transition</a>
  <h1>Left and Right Buttons </h1>
  <!-- This appears on the right -->
  <a href="info.html" data-icon="plus">Add</a>
</div>
```

Buttons can be moved to the left or right, as shown here:

```
<div data-role="header">
<a href="index.html" class="ui-btn-right">Right</a>
 <h1>Page title</h1>
<a href="info.html" class="ui-btn-left">Left</a>
</div>
```

Navigation Buttons as Anchor Links

In jQuery Mobile, the recommended practice is to define navigation buttons as anchor links and to define form submission buttons as button elements.

An anchor link that contains the attribute `data-role="button"` is styled as a button, as shown here:

```
<a href="external.html" data-role="button">Link-based button</a>
```

A jQuery Mobile button element or input element whose type is `submit`, `reset`, `button`, or `image` does not require the attribute `data-role="button"` because jQuery Mobile automatically treats these elements as a link-based button.

Although the original form-based button is not displayed, it is included in the HTML markup, and when a click event occurs on a link button, a corresponding click event occurs on the original form button.

Groups of Buttons and Column Grids

jQuery Mobile enables you to render a set of buttons (or checkboxes or radio buttons) as a block by defining a container HTML `<div>` element that specifies the attribute `data-role="controlgroup"`, and then include one or more button elements. The default rendering of the included buttons is horizontal (a row), and you can render the buttons as a vertical group by specifying the attribute `data-type="vertical"`.

jQuery Mobile renders the buttons, removes margins (and drop shadows) between buttons, and also "rounds" the first and last buttons in order to create a group-like effect. The following code block shows you how to specify a horizontal group of buttons:

```
<div data-role="controlgroup">
  <a href="index1.html" data-role="button">One</a>
  <a href="index2.html" data-role="button">Two</a>
  <a href="index3.html" data-role="button">Three</a>
</div>
```

One point to keep in mind: the buttons will "wrap" to additional rows if the number of buttons exceeds the screen width. Listing 8.5 shows you how to render a horizontal group and a vertical group of buttons.

The jQuery Mobile framework enables you to render CSS-based columns through a block style class convention called `ui-grid`. You can render two-column, three-column, four-column, and five-column layouts by using the class value `ui-grid-a`, `ui-grid-b`, `ui-grid-c`, and `ui-grid-d`, respectively. The following code block illustrates how to render a two-column layout:

```
<div class="ui-grid-a">
  <div class="ui-block-a">Block 1 and text inside will wrap</div>
  <div class="ui-block-b">Block 2 and text inside will wrap</div>
</div>
```

Notice the difference in the following code block that displays a three-column layout:

```
<div class="ui-grid-b">
  <div class="ui-block-a">Block 1 and text inside will wrap</div>
  <div class="ui-block-b">Block 2 and text inside will wrap</div>
  <div class="ui-block-c">Block 3 and text inside will wrap</div>
</div>
```

You can find more details and code samples here:

http://jquerymobile.com/demos/1.0b1/#/demos/1.0/docs/content/content-grids.html

Rendering Buttons with Themes

jQuery Mobile has an extensive theming system involving themes, labeled "a" through "e," for controlling the manner in which buttons are styled. When a link is added to a container, jQuery Mobile will assign it a theme "swatch" letter that matches the theme of its parent. For example, a button placed inside a content container with a theme of "a" (black in the default theme) is automatically assigned the button theme of "a" (charcoal in the default theme).

An example of a button theme is shown here:

```
<div data-role="footer" class="ui-bar">
 <a href="left.html" data-icon="arrow-l"
    data-role="button" data-theme="a">Left</a>
</div>
```

Listing 8.5 displays the contents of `JQMButtons1.html`, which illustrates how to render buttons horizontally and vertically, how to apply different themes, and how to specify custom CSS selectors.

LISTING 8.5: JQMButtons1.html

```
<!DOCTYPE html>
<html lang="en">
  <head>
    <meta charset="utf-8" />
    <title>Multiple Buttons and Themes in jQuery Mobile</title>

    <link rel="stylesheet" href="CSS3Background1.css" />

    <link rel="stylesheet"
    href="http://code.jquery.com/mobile/1.1.0/jquery.mobile-
1.1.0.min.css" />
    <script src="http://code.jquery.com/jquery-2.0.0b1.js">
    </script>
    <script src="http://code.jquery.com/jquery-migrate-1.1.0.js">
    </script>

    <script src="http://code.jquery.com/mobile/1.1.0/jquery.mobile-
1.1.0.min.js">
    </script>
  </head>
```

```
<body>
  <div id="page1" data-role="page">
    <div data-role="header">
      <!-- This button appears on the left -->
      <a href="abc.html" data-icon="arrow-l" data-theme="b">Index</a>

      <h1>Rendering Buttons in jQuery Mobile</h1>

      <!-- This button appears on the right -->
      <a href="def.html" data-icon="plus" data-theme="e">Add</a>
    </div>

    <div class="content" data-role="content">
      <div data-role="controlgroup" data-type="horizontal">
        <a href="index1.html" data-role="button">One</a>
        <a href="index2.html" data-role="button">Two</a>
        <a href="index3.html" data-role="button">Three</a>
        <a href="index4.html" data-role="button">Four</a>
        <a href="index5.html" data-role="button">Five</a>
      </div>

        <a href="index6.html" class="shadow"
           data-role="button">Vertical1</a>
        <a href="index7.html" class="shadow"
           data-role="button">Vertical2</a>
        <a href="index8.html" class="shadow"
           data-role="button">Vertical3</a>

      <div data-role="controlgroup">
        <a href="index6.html" data-role="button">Vertical1</a>
        <a href="index7.html" data-role="button">Vertical2</a>
        <a href="index8.html" data-role="button">Vertical3</a>
      </div>

      <div>
        <a href="index9.html" data-role="button"  id="cancel"
           data-inline="true">Cancel</a>
        <a href="index10.html" data-role="button" id="submit"
           data-inline="true" data-theme="b">Save</a>
      </div>
    </div>

    <!-- Display four directional array keys -->
    <div data-role="footer" class="ui-bar">
     <a href="left.html" data-icon="arrow-l"
        data-role="button" data-theme="a">Left</a>
     <a href="up.html" data-icon="arrow-u"
        data-role="button" data-theme="b">Up</a>
     <a href="down.html" data-icon="arrow-d"
        data-role="button" data-theme="c">Down</a>
     <a href="right.html" data-icon="arrow-r"
        data-role="button"data-theme="e">Right</a>
    </div>

  </div>
 </body>
</html>
```

Listing 8.5 contains HTML markup and references to jQuery files, followed by a single page view that renders an assortment of buttons (they have a `data-role="button"` attribute), some of which are in a horizontal group, and others are in a vertical group.

Notice that the vertical group of buttons are rendered with a reddish-tinged background shadow, which creates a richer visual effect, simply by specifying a value of `shadow` for the `class` attribute, as shown in bold in this code block:

```
<a href="index6.html" class="shadow" data-role="button">Vertical1</a>
<a href="index7.html" class="shadow" data-role="button">Vertical2</a>
<a href="index8.html" class="shadow" data-role="button">Vertical3</a>
```

In addition, the "cancel" and "submit" buttons specify class="shadow", and they are rendered with a psychedelic effect, which you obviously don't want to render in most cases. Nevertheless, you see how easily you can style buttons with custom CSS3-based visual effects, and the definition of the `shadow` selector is shown in Listing 8.6.

The bottom row of four HTML `<a>` elements in Listing 8.5 renders four directional arrows because they have a `data-icon` attribute that is set to `arrow-l`, `arrow-u`, `arrow-d`, and `arrow-r`, respectively. In addition, these four HTML `<a>` elements specify different values for the attribute data-theme, and they are rendered according to the visual display for each of these pre-defined jQuery Mobile themes.

Note that the HTML `<a>` elements in Listing 8.6 reference HTML Web pages that are not defined for this mobile application, so when users click on these links, they will see an error message.

LISTING 8.6: CSS3Background1.css
```
#cancel, #submit, .shadow {
 background-color:white;
 background-image:
  -webkit-radial-gradient(red 4px, transparent 18px),
  -webkit-repeating-radial-gradient(red 2px,  green 4px,
                                    yellow 8px, blue 12px,
                                    transparent 28px,
                                    green 20px, red 24px,
                                    transparent 28px,
                                    transparent 32px),
  -webkit-repeating-radial-gradient(red 2px,  green 4px,
                                    yellow 8px, blue 12px,
                                    transparent 28px,
                                    green 20px, red 24px,
                                    transparent 28px,
                                    transparent 32px);

 background-size: 50px 60px, 70px 80px;
 background-position: 0 0;
 -webkit-box-shadow:  30px 30px 30px #400;
}
```

Listing 8.6 contains definitions that are familiar to you from Chapter 2, and you can refer to the relevant sections in that chapter if you need to refresh your memory.

Figure 8.6 displays the result of rendering the HTML Web page in Listing 8.5 on a Sprint Nexus S 4G with Android ICS.

As you can see, there are many styling-related options available in jQuery mobile, so a summary of the discussion about jQuery Mobile buttons might be helpful:

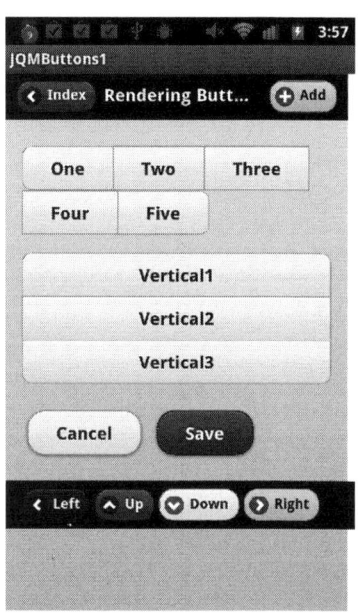

FIGURE 8.6 Buttons on a Sprint Nexus S 4G with Android ICS.

- an anchor link with the attribute data-role="button" is rendered as a button
- any input element where the type button, submit, reset, or image is assigned a class of `ui-btn-hidden` and a link-based button is displayed
- add a `data-icon` attribute to create a button with an icon
- add a `data-iconpos` attribute to change the position of the icon
- specify `data-inline="true"` to render a button only as wide as its text
- `data-role="controlgroup"` (`data-type="horizontal"`) groups buttons vertically (horizontally) in a `<div>` element
- `data-theme="e"` attribute is the fifth of five jQuery themes ("a" through "e")

LIST VIEWS IN JQUERY MOBILE

jQuery Mobile supports list views (which are very common in mobile applications), and several variations, including list view buttons, nested list views, and list view split buttons. jQuery Mobile can enhance ordered lists and unordered lists by applying the attribute `data-role="listview"` to a list. List view elements that are embedded inside anchor tags, respond to user gestures, as shown in Listing 8.7, which displays the contents of the jQuery Mobile Web page JQMSimpleListView1.html.

LISTING 8.7 JQMSimpleListView1.html
```
<!DOCTYPE html>
<html lang="en">
  <head>
    <meta charset=utf-8" />
    <title>Simple List Views in jQuery Mobile</title>
```

```
  <link rel="stylesheet"
   href="http://code.jquery.com/mobile/1.1.0/jquery.mobile-
1.1.0.min.css" />
  <script src="http://code.jquery.com/jquery-2.0.0b1.js">
  </script>
  <script src="http://code.jquery.com/jquery-migrate-1.1.0.js">
  </script>
   <script src="http://code.jquery.com/mobile/1.1.0/jquery.mobile-
1.1.0.min.js">
  </script>
  </head>

  <body>
    <div data-role="page">
      <div data-role="header"> <h2>This is the Header</h2> </div>
      <div data-role="content">
        <h3>Simple Unordered List Example</h3>
        <ul data-role="listview">
          <li><a href="#">Unordered Item 1</a></li>
          <li><a href="#">Unordered Item 2</a></li>
          <li><a href="#">Unordered Item 3</a></li>
        </ul>
        <h3>Simple Ordered List Example</h3>
        <ol data-role="listview">
          <li><a href="#">Ordered Item 1</a></li>
          <li><a href="#">Ordered Item 2</a></li>
          <li><a href="#">Ordered Item 3</a></li>
        </ol>
      </div>
      <div data-role="footer"> <h2>This is the Footer</h2> </div>
    </div>
  </body>
</html>
```

Whenever users tap on any list item in Listing 8.7, you can detect that event and execute custom code (if any) that you have bound to that event. In this example, the `href` attribute has value #, so the page is reloaded when users tap or click on the list items.

Figure 8.7 displays the result of rendering the HTML Web page in Listing 8.7 in landscape mode on a Nexus 7 2 tablet with Android JellyBean 4.3.

Additional Code Samples on the DVD

jQuery Mobile can create interactive views with nested lists, and users can "drill down" by tapping on list items. The first view displays the items in the top-level list, and tapping on one of those items will display the sub-list for that item (and so forth). In

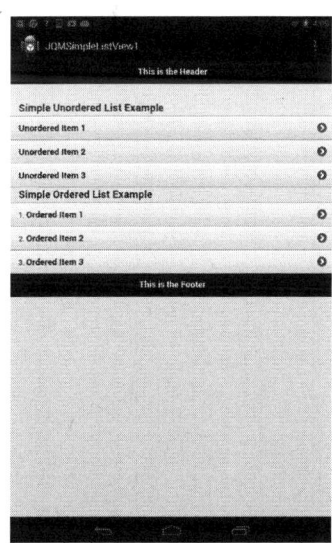

FIGURE 8.7 List View on a Nexus 7 2 Tablet with Android JellyBean 4.3.

addition, jQuery Mobile automatically provides a back button and also takes care of the URL mapping and transitions between pages.

The HTML5 Web page JQMNestedListViews1.html on the DVD is a jQuery Mobile Web page that illustrates how to render nested lists and how to navigate between pages when users click on list items.

Navigation bars in mobile applications often consist of a set of buttons that enable users to navigate through the page views. jQuery Mobile allows you to include navigation bars in the header, footer, or content areas of a page view (and also provide the appropriate formatting for the navigation bars).

To designate a navigation bar, apply the data-role="navigation" to a block level element like the HTML5 <nav> element. Anchor tags contained within a designated navigation element will be formatted as a button group, and jQuery Mobile will handle changing the active and inactive states of the buttons automatically, as shown in the HTML5 Web page JQMNavigation-Bar1.html on the DVD.

jQuery Mobile enables you to show and hide a list of menu options, and you can also use transitions to create animation effects as the menu list is displayed or hidden from view. The HTML5 Web page JQMMenu1.html on the DVD illustrates how to create a sliding menu in an HTML5 Web page.

jQuery Mobile and Ajax

jQuery Mobile uses Ajax for form submission, and will attempt to integrate the server response into the DOM of the application, providing transitions as expected. If you wish to prevent jQuery Mobile from using Ajax to handle a form, apply the attribute data-ajax="false" to the form tag.

Listing 8.8 displays the contents of JQMAjax1.html that illustrates how to handle Ajax invocations in a jQuery Mobile application.

LISTING 8.8: JQMAjax1.html

```
<!DOCTYPE html>
<html lang="en">
<head>
    <meta charset="utf-8" />
    <title>jQuery Mobile and AJAX</title>


    <link rel="stylesheet"
     href="http://code.jquery.com/mobile/1.1.0/jquery.mobile-
1.1.0.min.css" />
    <script
      src="http://code.jquery.com/jquery-2.0.0b1.js">
    </script>
    <script
      src="http://code.jquery.com/jquery-migrate-1.1.0.js">
    </script>

    <script
src="http://code.jquery.com/mobile/1.1.0/jquery.mobile-1.1.0.min.js">
    </script>
  </head>
```

```
    <body>
      <script>
       var xmlData = "", count = 0;

       $("#page1").live('pageinit', (function(event){
         $.ajax({
           url: 'http://localhost:8080/sample.xml',
           dataType: 'xml',
           success: function(data) {
                     $(data)
                        .find('svg')
                        .children()
                        .each(function() {
                          var node = $(this);
                          var x        = node.attr('x');
                          var y        = node.attr('y');
                          var width  = node.attr('width');
                          var height = node.attr('height');
                          var stroke = node.attr('stroke');
                          var fill   = node.attr('fill');

                          // other processing here...
                          ++count;

                          console.log("element: "+node);
                        });
                        console.log("element count: "+count);
           },
           error: function() {
             alert('no data found');
           }
         })
       })
       );
      </script>

      <div id="page1" data-role="page">
        <div data-role="header">Header</div>
        <div data-role="content">
          <p>Hello World from jQuery Mobile</p>
        </div>
        <div data-role="footer">Footer</div>
      </div>
    </body>
</html>
```

Listing 8.8 contains HTML markup and a jQuery Mobile Ajax invocation that is executed after this Web page is loaded into a browser, after which the code processes all the child elements of the <svg> element in the XML document sample.xml (displayed in Listing 8.9), as shown here:

```
var node = $(this);
var x        = node.attr('x');
var y        = node.attr('y');
var width  = node.attr('width');
```

```
var height = node.attr('height');
var stroke = node.attr('stroke');
var fill   = node.attr('fill');
```

For the purpose of illustration, this code makes the assumption that the XML document `sample.xml` in Listing 8.9 contains XML elements that have the attributes specified in the preceding code block.

LISTING 8.9: sample.xml

```
<?xml version='1.0' encoding='iso-8859-1'?>
<svg xmlns="http://www.w3.org/2000/svg"
     xmlns:xlink="http://www.w3.org/1999/xlink"
     width="100%" height="100%">
  <rect x="50"  y="10" width="100" height="200"
        stroke="blue" fill="red" />
  <rect x="200" y="10" width="100" height="200"
        stroke="blue" fill="green" />
  <rect x="350" y="10" width="100" height="200"
        stroke="blue" fill="blue" />
</svg>
```

Place the files in Listings 8.8 and 8.9 in the same directory, and launch a Web server that serves requests on port 8080. Launch the HTML Web page in Listing 8.8 in a Chrome browser on a laptop or desktop, open Chrome Inspector, and inspect the contents of the Chrome console. You will see something similar to the contents of Figure 8.8, which displays the contents of the Chrome Inspector in a Chrome browser on a Macbook.

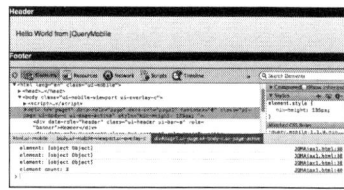

FIGURE 8.8 A jQuery Mobile Ajax Invocation on a Chrome Browser on a Macbook.

JQUERY MOBILE AND GEOLOCATION

In Chapter 5, you learned how to obtain Geolocation information for users. In this section, you will see how to use jQuery Mobile in order to obtain Geolocation information.

Listing 8.10 displays the contents of `JQMGeoLocation1.html` that illustrates how to obtain Geolocation information in an HTML5 Web page.

LISTING 8.10: JQMGeoLocation1.html

```
<!DOCTYPE html>
<html lang="en">
<head>
  <meta charset="utf-8">
  <title>JQueryMobile Geolocation</title>

  <link rel="stylesheet"
   href="http://code.jquery.com/mobile/1.1.0/jquery.mobile-
1.1.0.min.css" />
```

```
    <script src="http://code.jquery.com/jquery-2.0.0b1.js">
    </script>
    <script src="http://code.jquery.com/jquery-migrate-1.1.0.js">
    </script>
    <script src="http://code.jquery.com/mobile/1.1.0/jquery.mobile-
1.1.0.min.js">
    </script>

    <!-- google maps API -->
    <script
      src="http://maps.google.com/maps/api/js?sensor=false">
    </script>

    <style>
#theMap, #theCoords {
font-size: 16px;
height: 200px;
width:  400px;
}
    </style>

<script>
    function findUserLocation() {
      // specify the 'success' and 'fail' JavaScript functions
      navigator.geolocation.getCurrentPosition(successCallback,
                                              errorCallback);
    }

function successCallback(position) {
  var latitude  = position.coords.latitude;
  var longitude = position.coords.longitude;
  var latlong   = new google.maps.LatLng(latitude, longitude);

  var myOptions = {
      zoom: 14,
      center: latlong,
      mapTypeId: google.maps.MapTypeId.ROADMAP
  };

  // use Google Maps to display the current location
  var map = new google.maps.Map(document.getElementById("theMap"),
myOptions);
  map.setCenter(latlong);

/*
    var marker = new google.maps.Marker({
      position: initialLocation,
      map: map,
      title: "I Am Here!"
  });
*/

  // display position details in the console
  positionDetails(position);
}
```

```
function errorCallback(error) {
  if(error.code = error.PERMISSION_DENIED) {
    console.log("Error: you must enable geolocation access");
  } else if(error.code = error.PERMISSION_UNAVAILABLE) {
    console.log("Error: geolocation unavailable");
  } else if(error.code = error.TIMEOUT) {
    console.log("Error: timeout occurred");
  }

//console.log(error);
}

function positionDetails(pos) {
 var positionStr =
    "Latitude:"+ pos.coords.latitude +"<br>"+
    "Longitude:"+ pos.coords.longitude +"<br>"+
    "Accuracy:"+ pos.coords.accuracy +"<br>"+

    "Altitude:"+ pos.coords.altitude +"<br>"+
    "AltitudeAccuracy:"+ pos.coords.altitudeAccuracy +"<br>"+
    "Heading:"+ pos.coords.heading +"<br>"+
    "Speed:"+ pos.coords.speed +"";

    $("#theCoords").html(positionStr);
    console.log(positionStr);
}
</script>
</head>

 <body>
    <div data-role="page" id="page1">
      <div data-role="header"><h3>JQuery Mobile Geolocation</div>
      <div data-role="content" id="content">
        <div id="theMap"> </div>

        <form id="geoLocationForm">
          <input type="button" id="geobutton"
                 value="Click to Find My Current Location">
        </form>
        <div id="theCoords"> </div>
      </div>
      <div data-role="footer"><h3>Footer</h3></div>
    </div>

    <script>
      $("#page1").live('pageinit', (function(event){
        $("#geobutton").bind("vmousedown",function(event, ui){
          findUserLocation();
        });
      })
      );
    </script>
  </body>
</html>
```

Listing 8.10 contains code that is very similar to the code sample that you saw in Chapter 5. The only difference is that the code in Listing 8.10 has been adapted to jQuery Mobile, whereas the code in Chapter 5 uses jQuery. As such, you can read the explanation that is provided immediately after the related code sample in Chapter 5.

Note: Make sure that you enable Geolocation on your mobile device.

If you are interested in mobile maps, there are many such examples available, including the details on this Website:

http://jquery-ui-map.googlecode.com/svn/trunk/demos/jquery-google-maps-mobile.html

SUMMARY

In this chapter, you learned about various features of jQuery Mobile, along with code samples that showed you examples of how to handle events, create Web pages with multiple page views, and how to create forms with HTML widgets. You also saw how to use CSS3 shadow and gradient effects (which you learned in Chapter 3) to style buttons in jQuery Mobile Web pages. You learned how to do the following in HTML Web pages that use jQuery Mobile:

- Render buttons
- Display simple and nested lists
- Render sliding menus
- Use jQuery Mobile with Ajax
- Use jQuery Mobile with Geolocation

OTHER HTML5 TECHNOLOGIES

This chapter provides an overview of several HTML5-related technologies and code samples for many of these technologies. Although you can use the HTML5 technologies in this chapter without jQuery (you can find online tutorials with that information), jQuery with HTML5 is a major aspect of this book, so the discussion of jQuery plugins for various HTML5 technologies in this chapter makes sense. Keep in mind that new jQuery plugins are continually being written, so it's worth comparing the latest jQuery plugins with the plugins that are covered in this chapter, and then you can decide which ones are best suited for your specific requirements.

The HTML5 technologies in this chapter are presented according to their W3C status: W3C Recommendation (REC), Candidate Recommendation (CR), Last Call (LC), Working Draft (WD), and experimental APIs. The HTML5 technologies in each section are presented alphabetically. This approach enables you to quickly determine the status of each HTML5 technology, which is the main advantage over using a pure alphabetical listing of HTML5 technologies.

The first part of this chapter briefly describes the stages of the W3C process, after which you will discover that the only two HTML5 technologies in the REC status are SVG (covered in an Appendix) and MathML (which is not covered in this book).

The second part of this chapter contains the HTML5 technologies with a W3C CR status, which includes GeoLocation, WebSockets, and XHR2. The Vibration API is discussed in Chapter 6 as part of the media portion of the chapter. The XHR2 section contains three Ajax-related examples, starting with a generic Ajax code sample, followed by a jQuery-based Ajax code sample. You will then learn about CORS, after which the code sample that uses Ajax with XHR2 (XmlHTTPRequest2) will make sense.

Next, you will see a jQuery-based code sample that illustrates drag and drop for JPG files (which is simpler than "pure" HTML5 Drag-and-Drop APIs), an example of invoking some of the HTML5 file APIs in jQuery, and finally a jQuery plugin for obtaining Geolocation information about users. You will also learn about the jQuery plugins `jStorage` and `jStore` that provide a layer of abstraction on top of the HTML5 Storage APIs.

The third part of this chapter presents HTML5 technologies whose W3C status is LC, which includes HTML5 Contacts, Drag-and-Drop (DnD), Web Messaging, and SSE.

The fourth part of this chapter provides an overview of HTML5 technologies whose W3C status is WD, which includes Audio Processing, HTML5 File APIs, Web Intents, Microdata, Web Notifications, WAI ARIA, Web Workers, History APIs, and Offline Web Applications. The final portion of this chapter covers the experimental HTML5 technologies, which includes Firefox OS (formerly B2G) and Voice Recognition (TTS).

This chapter also contains information about jQuery plugins that are available for various HTML5 technologies because it's often easier to use jQuery plugins than the underlying HTML5 APIs, which are presented in broad brushstrokes. However, if you do decide to use jQuery plugins, you also need to consider the tradeoffs that are involved, such as greater file size overhead, performance differences, and memory footprint for smaller devices that may affect your decision to use jQuery, jQuery Mobile, or other toolkits in your Web applications. Moreover, loading extra files might also load more code than you actually need, and there is also the maintenance aspect (such as keeping up with version changes) for your code.

If you have the choice (and perhaps the "luxury"), you probably prefer ease of coding instead of getting "bogged down" in long and tedious code samples when there are simpler alternatives available. For example, the code sample that uses jQuery for HTML5 Drag-andDrop (DnD) is much more straightforward than a code sample that directly invokes the existing HTML5 DnD APIs.

The other advantage of simpler code samples is that they will quickly introduce you to a number of HTML5 technologies, after which you will be in a better position to explore the nuances of those HTML5 technologies. Another scenario is to combine jQuery Mobile with other toolkits, such as PhoneGap (discussed in Chapter 3) or appMobi (which is not discussed in this book). Toolkits such as PhoneGap provide support for hardware functionality, and you can also combine PhoneGap with jQuery Mobile. Your application requirements and constraints will determine your choice of toolkits (if any) for your mobile Web applications.

In general, jQuery and jQuery Mobile will probably work with other toolkits, but you ought to check online forums for any issues that might affect your Web applications. Finally, if you prefer not to use jQuery plugins, you can perform an Internet search to find online tutorials that illustrate how to create

HTML5 Web pages using pure HTML5 APIs for all the HTML5 technologies that are covered in this book.

THE STAGES IN THE W3C REVIEW PROCESS

If you are unfamiliar with the various stages of the W3C process, the following brief description (from earliest stage to final stage) is provided below.

A WD ("Working Draft") document is the first form of a standard that is publicly available, and comments are widely accepted (but not guaranteed to be incorporated), and this document could differ significantly from its final form.

A LC ("Last Call") status involves the creation of a public record of the responses of a working group to all comments about a specification. This stage also handles bug reports about a specification. Incidentally, HTML5 reached the LC status in the W3C in May of 2011.

A CR ("Candidate Recommendation") status is more firm than the WD document (major features have been finalized), and the goal is to elicit assistance from the development community regarding the extent to which the standard can be implemented.

A PR ("Proposed Recommendation") status means that the standard has passed two previous stages, and at this point the document is submitted to the W3C for final approval.

A REC ("Recommendation") status is the final stage of a ratification process, comparable to a published technical standard in many other industries. The criterion for the specification becoming a W3C Recommendation is "two 100% complete and fully interoperable implementations."

Recall that Chapter 1 describes some of the groups that create specifications, with detailed information about APIs for the technologies that are discussed in this chapter.

HTML5 APIS IN W3C RECOMMENDATION STATUS (REC)

This section of the chapter contains a set of HTML5 APIs that have Recommendation status. You might be surprised to discover that SVG and MathML are the only two technologies with REC status. Both of these technologies are mature and they are included under the HTML5 umbrella. You can read about SVG in an Appendix, whereas MathML 3.0 is not covered in this book.

HTML5 APIS IN W3C CANDIDATE RECOMMENDATION STATUS (CR)

This section of the chapter contains a set of HTML5 APIs that have Candidate Recommendation status. Although the HTML5 technologies Navigation Timing, RDFa, and Selectors have CR status, they are not discussed in this book.

XMLHTTPREQUEST LEVEL 2 (XHR2)

The `XMLHttpRequest` Level 2 specification supports the following new features:

- Handling byte streams such as File, Blob and FormData objects for upload and download
- showing Progress events during upload and download
- making Cross-origin requests
- making anonymous requests (not HTTP Referer)
- setting a Timeout for the Request

Before we look at an XHR2 code sample, we'll start with a code sample that shows you how to make a simple Ajax request, followed by an Ajax request that uses jQuery. Next you will learn about CORS, and the final portion of this section discusses XHR2.

Making Ajax Calls with jQuery

This example contains several jQuery methods that provide Ajax-based functionality, including `jQuery.load()`, `jQuery.get()`, and `jQuery.post()`, and `jQuery.ajax()`.

Listing 9.1 displays the contents of `JQueryAjax1.html` that illustrates how to use the first of these jQuery Ajax methods in an HTML Web page in order to read the contents of an XML document.

LISTING 9.1: JQueryAjax1.html

```
<!DOCTYPE html>
<html>
<head>
 <meta charset="utf-8" >
 <title>JQuery Ajax</title>

 <script src="http://code.jquery.com/jquery-2.0.0b1.js">
 </script>
 <script src="http://code.jquery.com/jquery-migrate-1.1.0.js">
 </script>

 <script>
  var url = "http://localhost:8080/sample.xml";

  $(document).ready(function() {
    $("#myDiv").load(url, function() {});
  });
 </script>
</head>

<body>
  <div id="myDiv"></div>
</body>
</html>
```

Listing 9.1 contains a mere one line of code that performs an Ajax request via the jQuery `load()` method, as shown here:

```
$("#myDiv").load(url, function() {});
```

Launch Listing 9.1 in a Web browser, after which the contents of the HTML `<div>` element whose `id` attribute is `myDiv` is replaced with the contents of `sample.xml` and three SVG-based rectangles are rendered.

Alternatively, you can use the `jQuery.ajax()` method as shown here:

```
$.ajax({
        url:  url,
        type: "get",
        success: GotData,
        dataType: 'xml'
});
```

In the preceding code block, you also need to define a JavaScript function called `GotData()` where you would process the result of the Ajax invocation.

As you would expect, jQuery provides much more Ajax functionality. Specifically, jQuery provides support for the following callback hooks:

```
beforeSend()
fail()
dataFilter()
done()
always()
```

The functions `beforeSend()`, `error()`, and `done()` are intuitively named and they behave as expected. The `dataFilter()` callback is the first callback to receive data; after it performs its processing, the `done()` callback is invoked. Finally, the `always()` callback is invoked, regardless of whether the result of the Ajax invocation was successful or in error.

A concise example of jQuery code that makes an Ajax request using method chaining with several of the preceding APIs is here:

```
// Assign handlers immediately after making the request,
// and get a reference to the jqxhr object for this request
var jqxhr = $.ajax( "example.php" )
   .done(function() { alert("success"); })
   .fail(function() { alert("error"); })
   .always(function() { alert("complete"); });

// perform other work here ...

// Set another completion function for the request above
jqxhr.always(function() { alert("second complete"); });
```

If you want to explore more Ajax-related features in jQuery, a complete list of jQuery Ajax methods is here:

http://api.jquery.com/category/ajax/
http://api.jquery.com/ajaxComplete/

This chapter contains one more Ajax-based code sample that users XHR2, but first we need to discuss CORS and some of the features that it provides in HTML5.

HTML5 CROSS ORIGIN RESOURCE SHARING (CORS)

Browsers base much of their security on the "origin": a combination of the scheme (e.g., http vs. https), hostname, and port number. The "same origin policy" permits the scripts on a page to communicate freely with the server that provided the page, but those scripts are restricted when communicating with other servers. In addition, if two Web pages have scripts from the same origin, a script on one Web page can manipulate the contents of the other Web page. Keep in mind that different browsers implement unique exceptions to the same-origin policy.

HTML5 defines a new policy called Cross-Origin Resource Sharing (CORS) that specifies how the browser should control access to resources when a Web page's origin and the requested item's origin are different. Although CORS is more flexible than "same origin policy," it does not remove all access controls. Instead, the browser enforces the same-origin policy, except where servers give permission for cross-origin access.

This permission happens by means of a simple header exchange between the browser and a server. (The browser could send a GET or OPTIONS request to a server and receive back an Access-Control-Allow-Origin header in the response. The browser will then let scripts make cross-origin requests to this server.)

Newer browsers have added CORS support to `XMLHttpRequest`. While this is a useful alternative to JSONP for cross-origin HTTP, the main use for CORS pertains to mixing protocols: using HTTP/HTTPS to get a Web page and then WebSockets (and Web Sockets Secure) to communicate with the server. Because different protocols lead to different origins, even with the same host, CORS is a necessity.

The best description of the same-origin policy is in Google's Browser Security Handbook at *http://code.google.com/p/browsersec/wiki/Part2#Same-origin_policy*.

For a more detailed description of CORS, see *http://enable-cors.org*.

Ajax Requests using `XMLHttpRequest` Level 2 (XHR2)

Listing 9.2 displays `AjaxForm.html`, which illustrates how to create an HTML5 Web page that uses the new `FormData` object XHR2.

LISTING 9.2 AjaxForm.html

```
<!doctype html>
<html lang="en">

<head>
 <meta charset="utf-8" >
 <title>Ajax Form</title>
```

```
<script>
  function sendForm(form) {
    var formData = new FormData(form);

    var xhr = new XMLHttpRequest();
    xhr.open('POST', form.action, true);
    xhr.onload = function(e) {
      // do something here
    };

    xhr.send(formData);

    // Prevent page submission
    return false;
  }
 </script>
</head>

<body>
<form id="myform" name="myform" action="xhr2.php">
  <input type="text"   name="uname" value="asmith">
  <input type="number" name="id"    value="33333">
  <input type="submit" onclick="return sendForm(this.form);">
</form>
</body>
</html>
```

Listing 9.2 is straightforward. The <body> element contains an HTML <form> element with several input fields. Next, the form data is submitted via the JavaScript function sendForm() that creates a FormData object and then submits the user-provided data via XHR2, as shown in this code block:

```
var xhr = new XMLHttpRequest();
xhr.open('POST', form.action, true);
xhr.onload = function(e) {
    // do something here
};
xhr.send(formData);
```

Two more points to know is that the XMLHttpRequest Level 2 specification supports the transfer of binary data and also the tracking of the upload progress through the XMLHttpRequestUpload object; consequently, XHR2 can be used for binary file transfers via the File APIs and the FormData object.

If you need to use XHR2 in your HTML Web pages, there is an XHR2 library here:

https://github.com/p-m-p/xhr2-lib

More tutorials and information regarding XHR2 are here:

http://www.html5rocks.com/en/tutorials/file/xhr2/
http://www.matiasmancini.com.ar/jquery-plugin-ajax-form-validation-html5.html

HTML5 APIS IN W3C LAST CALL STATUS (LC)

This section contains a set of HTML5 APIs that have Last Call status. The following HTML5 APIs also have LC status, most of which are discussed in Chapter 1:

- Audio and video
- HTML markup
- Web storage (Chapter 2)

The Canvas 2D APIs are discussed in an Appendix on the DVD.

HTML5 DRAG-AND-DROP (DND)

HTML5 Drag-and-Drop enables you to rearrange the layout of HTML elements in an HTML Web page. HTML4 does not have built-in support for DnD, and creating such support requires considerably more JavaScript code than a toolkit such as jQuery.

On the other hand, HTML5 provides Drag-and-Drop APIs that support Drag-and-Drop in HTML5 Web pages. HTML5 Drag-and-Drop supports the following events:

```
drag
dragend
dragenter
dragleave
dragover
dragstart
drop
```

In addition, the HTML5 DnD provides a source element, the data content, and the target, which represent the drag "start" element, the data that is being dragged, and the "target" element, respectively.

In your HTML5 Web page, you attach event listeners to elements, as shown here:

```
myElement.addEventListener('dragenter', handleDragEnter, false);
myElement.addEventListener('dragleave', handleDragLeave, false);
myElement.addEventListener('dragover',  handleDragOver,  false);
myElement.addEventListener('dragstart', handleDragStart, false);
```

Next, you define custom code in each of the JavaScript event handlers that will be executed whenever the associated event occurs.

However, keep in mind that HTML5 Web pages with DnD functionality still require browser-specific code, which means that you need to maintain the code in multiple HTML5 Web pages if you want to support multiple browsers.

HTML5 Drag-and-Drop is probably one of the most tedious of the HTML5 APIs, and Peter Paul Koch of "QuirksMode" fame expresses his thoughts regarding DnD in one of his blog posts (please note that there is strong language here):

http://www.quirksmode.org/blog/archives/2009/09/the_html5_drag.html

Eric Bidelman has written an extensive and detailed blog entry that shows you how to write an HTML5 Web page with Drag-and-Drop functionality:

http://www.html5rocks.com/en/tutorials/dnd/basics/

We will skip examples of "native" HTML5 DnD and proceed to an example of using jQuery with HTML5 DnD, which is covered in the next section.

JQUERY AND HTML5 DRAG-AND-DROP

Drag-and-Drop is exceptionally simple in jQuery: only one line of code is required for an HTML element.

Listing 9.3 displays the contents of the HTML5 Web page JQDragAnd-Drop1.html, which illustrates how easy it is to create an HTML5 Web page with Drag-and-Drop using jQuery.

LISTING 9.3 JQDragAndDrop1.html

```
<!doctype html>
<html lang="en">
<head>
 <meta charset="utf-8" >
 <title>JQuery DnD</title>

<style>
 div[id^="draggable"] {
   position:relative; width: 100px; height: 100px;
 }

 #draggable1 { background: red; }
 #draggable2 { background: yellow; }
 #draggable3 { background: blue; }
</style>

<script src="http://code.jquery.com/jquery-2.0.0b1.js">
 </script>
<script src="http://code.jquery.com/jquery-migrate-1.1.0.js">
</script>

<script src="http://ajax.googleapis.com/ajax/libs/jqueryui/1.10.1/
jquery-ui.min.js">
</script>

<script
  $(document).ready(function() {
    $('#draggable1').draggable();
    $('#draggable2').draggable();
    $('#draggable3').draggable();
  });
</script>
</head>
```

```
<body>
  <div id="content" style="height: 400px;">
    <div id="draggable1">
        <img src="Sample1.png" width="100" height="100" />
    </div>
    <div id="draggable2">
        <img src="Sample2.png" width="100" height="100" />
    </div>
    <div id="draggable3">
        <img src="Sample3.png" width="100" height="100" />
    </div>
  </div>
</body>
</html>
```

Listing 9.3 contains a block of jQuery code that makes three HTML `<div>` elements (which are defined in the `<body>` element) draggable using this type of code snippet:

```
$('#draggable2').draggable();
```

The `<body>` element contains three `<div>` elements, each of which contains a PNG image that you can drag around the screen.

Figure 9.1 displays the result of rendering Listing 9.3 in a Chrome browser on a Macbook.

Figure 9.2 shows an example of dragging the images in Listing 9.3 to different positions in a Chrome browser on a Macbook.

More information about jQuery Drag-and-Drop (including the list of available options) is available here:

http://jqueryui.com/demos/draggable/

There are several jQuery plug-ins for drag-and-drop functionality that are listed here:

http://plugins.jquery.com/projects/plugins?type=45

You can also use jQuery Mobile with HTML5 DnD, and although we will not discuss an example (due to space constraints), you can perform an Internet search to find tutorials and code examples, or you can start with the details in this link:

http://www.jsplugins.com/Scripts/ Plugins/View/Jquery-Mobile-Drag- And-Drop/

FIGURE 9.1 Three Images in a Chrome Browser on a Macbook.

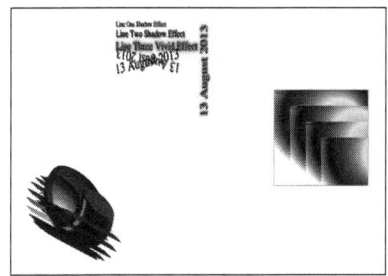

FIGURE 9.2 Three Dragged Images in a Chrome Browser on a Macbook.

JQUERY AND HTML5 LOCAL STORAGE

Chapter 1 discusses HTML5 local storage, and this section introduces you to jQuery plugins that provide a layer of abstraction over local storage and session storage.

The jQuery plugin jStorage is a cross-browser plugin that enables you to use jQuery syntax in order to manage data in local storage, and its home page is here:

http://www.jstorage.info/

The JStorage APIs enable you to get, set, and delete data in storage; you can also check if storage is available, as well as the size of the stored data (in bytes). The intuitively named JStorage APIs are listed here for your convenience:

```
$.jStorage.set(key, value)
$.jStorage.get(key)
$.jStorage.deleteKey(key)
$.jStorage.flush()
$.jStorage.index()
$.jStorage.storageSize()
$.jStorage.currentBackend()
$.jStorage.reInit()
$.jStorage.storageAvailable()
```

Listing 9.4 displays the contents of JQJStorage1.html that illustrates how to use JStorage in order to save data in the storage area of your browser.

LISTING 9.4 JQJStorage1.html

```
<!DOCTYPE html>
<html lang="en">
  <head>
   <meta charset="utf-8" >
   <title>JStorage Example</title>

   <link rel="stylesheet"
    href="http://code.jquery.com/mobile/1.1.0/jquery.mobile-
1.1.0.min.css" />
    <script src="http://code.jquery.com/jquery-2.0.0b1.js"></
script>
    <script src="http://code.jquery.com/jquery-migrate-1.1.0.js"></
script>

    <script src="http://code.jquery.com/mobile/1.1.0/jquery.mobile-
1.1.0.min.js">
    </script>

    <script src="http://ajax.googleapis.com/ajax/libs/
jqueryui/1.10.1/jquery-ui.min.js">
    </script>
```

```
<script src="jstorage.js"></script>

  <script>
    $(document).ready(function() {
      // Check if "key" exists in the storage
      var value = $.jStorage.get("key");

      if(!value){
        // if not - load the data from the server
        value = load_data_from_server()

        // save the value
        $.jStorage.set("key",value);
      }
    });
  </script>
</head>

<body>
  <div> </div>
</body>
</html>
```

The core functionality in Listing 9.4 takes place in a short JavaScript code block with conditional logic that checks for the existence of a data item in local storage with the value key. If this value does not exist, then the `load_data_from_server()` JavaScript function (which is not shown) is invoked, and then the return value is stored in local storage.

You can also use the jQuery plugin `jStore` for HTML5 storage, which is a cross-browser plugin that enables you to use jQuery syntax in order to manage data in local storage, and its homepage is here:

http://code.google.com/p/jquery-jstore/source/browse/trunk/src/engines/ jStore.Html5.js?r=6

LIBRARIES FOR HTML5 LOCAL STORAGE

A number of JavaScript toolkits are available for local storage, some of which use jQuery (and some do not use jQuery). This short section briefly describes some of the available toolkits.

lscache emulates `memcache` functions using HTML5 localStorage for caching data in a client browser, along with an expiration time for each data item.

The `lscache` homepage is here:

https://github.com/pamelafox/lscache

If the localStorage limit (approximately 5MB) is exceeded, items that are closest to their expiration date are removed. If localStorage is unavailable, `lscache` does not cache anything (and all cache requests return null).

The `lscache` methods are `set()`, `get()`, `remove()`, and `flush()`, and a jQuery `lscache` plugin is available here:

https://github.com/mckamey

YQL LocalCache is a wrapper for YQL to support local storage, and its homepage is here:

https://github.com/phunkei/autoStorage

A sample invocation with YQL LocalCache with self-explanatory parameters is here:

```
yqlcache.get({
  yql: 'select * from flickr.photos.search where text="warsaw"',
  id: 'myphotos',
  cacheage: ( 60*60*1000 ),
  callback: function(data) {
    console.log(data);
  }
});
```

The returned data in the callback is an object with two properties: data (the YQL data) and type ('cached' for cached data or 'freshcache'). You can get additional code samples here:

https://github.com/codepo8/yql-localcache

Savify is a jQuery plugin for automatically recording a user's progress in a form while it is being completed, and its homepage is here:

https://github.com/blackcoat/Savify

HTML5 APIS IN W3C WORKING DRAFT STATUS (WD)

The HTML5 technologies in this section (listed in alphabetical order) currently have a "Working Draft" status. IndexedDB has WD status and it was discussed in Chapter 1, so we will not repeat that content here. In addition, the following HTML5 technologies also have WD status but they are not discussed in this chapter:

• Media Capture
• RDFa
• Touch Events

JQUERY AND HTML5 FILE APIS

The HTML5 File APIs enable you to create, read, and write files on the file system. The first step is to obtain access to the HTML5 FileSystem, after which you can perform file-related operations. You can read about these APIs and also see code examples here:

http://aquantum-demo.appspot.com/file-upload
http://www.htmlgoodies.com/html5/other/responding-to-html5-filereader-events.html

The DVD contains the HTML Web page JQFileInfo1.html that illustrates how to use jQuery in order to display the attributes of a file that is selected by users. A more interesting (and more useful) example is JQFile-Upload2.html in Listing 9.5 that illustrates how to use jQuery and XHR2 to upload files.

LISTING 9.5: JQFileUpload2.html

```
<!DOCTYPE HTML>
<html lang="en">
 <head>
   <meta charset="utf-8" >
   <title>JQuery File Upload</title>

   <script src="http://code.jquery.com/jquery-2.0.0b1.js">
   </script>

   <script
     src="http://code.jquery.com/jquery-migrate-1.1.0.js">
   </script>
 </head>

<body>
 <script>
   $(document).ready(function () {
     $("body").on("change", '#fileUploader', function() {
        // Prepare post data
        var data = new FormData();
        data.append('uploadfile', this.files[0]);

        // invoke the jQuery .ajax method:
        $.ajax({
          type: 'POST',
          url: url,
          data: data,
          success:  function(data) {
                      // do something here
                    },
          dataType: 'text'
        });
     });
   });
 </script>

 <div>
   <input id="fileUploader" type="file" multiple />
 </div>
 </body>
</html>
```

Listing 9.5 contains an HTML <input> field that enables users to select a file from the file system. After a file is selected, the jQuery "change" event is triggered, and an XHR2 FormData object (discussed earlier in this chapter) is created and populated, as shown here:

```
var data = new FormData();
data.append('uploadfile', this.files[0]);
```

The selected file is uploaded via the jQuery `.ajax()` method, which contains a "success" function that is invoked after the Ajax request has been completed successfully.

If you want to use a jQuery plugin for uploading files in HTML5 Web pages, there are several available, such as the cross-browser jQuery plugin `jquery-filedrop`, and its homepage is here:

https://github.com/weixiyen/jquery-filedrop

HTML5 HISTORY APIS

Prior to HTML5, the browser support for history-related APIs provided limited functionality. You could find the number of items in the browser history, move forward and backward, and several links backward, as shown here:

```
console.log(history.length);
console.log(history.forward());
console.log(history.back());
console.log(history.go(-2));
```

Several new APIs are available, as shown here:

```
history.pushState(data, title, url);
history.replaceState(data, title, url);
```

The parameters in the `history.pushState()` method are as follows:
`data` is some type of structured data, assigned to the history item
`title` is the name of the item in the history drop-down that is displayed by the browser's back and forward buttons
`url` is the (optional) URL that is displayed in the address bar
The parameters in the `history.replaceState()` method are the same as the `history.pushState()` method, except that the former updates information that is already in the browser's history.

In addition, there is the new `popstate` event, which occurs when users view their browser history, and you can use it in the following manner:

```
window.addEventListener("popstate", function(event) {
  // do something here
});
```

Keep in mind that different browsers implement HTML5 browser history in different ways, so the following JavaScript toolkit is useful:

https://github.com/balupton/History.js/

The `History.js` toolkit supports jQuery, MooTools and Prototype, and in HTML5 browsers you can modify the URL directly without resorting to hashes.

HTML5 OFFLINE WEB APPLICATIONS

The purpose of Offline Web Applications is simple: users can work on an application even when they are disconnected from the Internet. When users do have access to the Internet, their data changes are synchronized so that everything is in a consistent state.

A Website that contains demos, additional links, and tutorial-like information is here:

http://appcachefacts.info/

The HTML5 specification requires a so-called "manifest file" (with an "appcache" as the suggested suffix) that contains the following three sections:

CACHE (the list of files that are going to be cached)

NETWORK (the files that can only be accessed online)

FALLBACK (specifies the resource to display when users try to access non-cached resources)

As a simple example, Listing 9.6 displays the contents of a sample manifest file called MyApp.appcache.

LISTING 9.6 MyApp.appcache

```
CACHE MANIFEST
# Verson 1.0.0
CACHE:
Index.html
Cachedstuff.html
Mystyle.css
Myimage.jpg

NETWORK:
*
FALLBACK:
/ noncached.html
```

You must ensure that the manifest file is served with the following MIME type:

```
text/cache-manifest
```

Second, every Web page that uses offline functionality must reference the manifest file at the top of the Web page:

```
<html lang="en" manifest="mymanifest.manifest">
```

If you have a Web page that is hosted by a provider, you can verify that the Web page contains the correct MIME type by issuing the following type of command:

```
curl -I http://www.myprovider.com/mymanifest.manifest
```

DETECTING ONLINE AND OFFLINE STATUS

The simplest way to determine whether or not an application is offline in an HTML5 Web page is with the following code snippet:

```
if(navigator.hasOwnProperty(onLine)) {
  // application is online
} else {
  // application is offline
}
```

For mobile applications that use jQuery Mobile, you can use the following type of code block:

```
$(document).bind("offline", function() {
  // application is offline
}
```

Binding the offline event as shown in the preceding code block is useful for handling situations whereby an application goes offline while users are actively viewing an application.

In addition, you would send data to a server only when you are online, and store data locally via HTML5 LocalStorage when you are offline.

The jQuery plugin jquery-offline is a cross-browser plugin that enables you to use jQuery syntax for Offline Applications, and its homepage is here:

https://github.com/wycats/jquery-offline

SUMMARY

This chapter provided an overview of various HTML5 technologies and grouped them according to their current W3C status. These technologies include Ajax (XHR2), Drag-and-Drop, File APIs, and Offline Applications. In this chapter, you also saw code examples that used jQuery with Drag-and-Drop and for uploading files, as well as how to use a jQuery plugin with HTML5 storage.

MOBILE APPS AND INTERNET ACCESS

In previous chapters, you learned how to create HTML5 mobile applications for Android using Eclipse and HMTL5 mobile applications for iOS using Xcode. In this chapter, you will learn how to create hybrid HTML5 mobile applications that support Internet access.

The first part of this chapter contains a code sample involving an HTML5 Web page that contains a mixture of jQuery Mobile code and a JavaScript file from Apigee, which also provides the server-side functionality for storing data. This mobile application can retrieve data from a server as well as post new data to the same server.

The second part of this chapter contains a code sample that renders a 3D bar chart in HTML5 `Canvas`.

The code sample in the final part of this chapter shows you an example of retrieving data from an HTML5 Web Socket server and then rendering that data in a bar chart using HTML5 `Canvas`.

WORKING WITH APIGEE

This section provides an overview of the features of Apigee. You will also lean how to register for a free Apigee account, how to use the online tool for creating a project (such as the one that is used in Listing 10.1), and how to insert data into the objects that you create for your project.

Apigee hosts free training events throughout the United States. In addition, Apigee can arrange to conduct free training sessions at your company, which is an excellent and cost-effective way for you to learn about mobile-related topics. Visit the Apigee Website for additional details.

ACCESSING AN APIGEE SERVER FROM A MOBILE APPLICATION

The code sample in this section is simple but useful because you can use this code whenever you need to display a collection of items in a scrollable list. The same logic can be used when you need to display other types of data, such as pictures from a social networking site, tweets from Twitter, or restaurants that are in a particular zip code or within a certain radius of your location. These are just some of the ways that you can adapt the code in Listing 10.1 to your application requirements.

Listing 10.1 displays the contents of the HTML5 Web page `MyBooks1. html` that retrieves and displays a set of books from a user account that is registered with Apigee. Users can also create new books (identified by a title and an author) that they can post to the same user account.

The HTML page `MyBooks1.html` in Listing 10.1 illustrates how to retrieve a collection of books from a remote server and how to post new books to the same server.

LISTING 10.1 MyBooks1.html

```
<!DOCTYPE html>
<html>
  <head>
    <meta charset="utf-8">
    <title>My Book List</title>

    <link rel="stylesheet"
    href="http://code.jquery.com/mobile/1.1.0/jquery.mobile-
1.1.0.min.css" />
    <script
      src="http://code.jquery.com/jquery-2.0.0b1.js">
    </script>
    <script src="http://code.jquery.com/jquery-migrate-1.1.0.js"></
script>

    <script
    src="http://code.jquery.com/mobile/1.1.1/jquery.mobile-
1.1.1.min.js">
    </script>

    <script
    src="http://raw.github.com/apigee/usergrid-javascript-sdk/
master/usergrid.min.js">
    </script>

    <script>
      // STEP 1: specify account information on Apigee
      var apigee = new Usergrid.Client({
        // specify the org name of your Usergrid
        // or apigee.com username for App Services
        orgName:'oswald',
        // Your Usergrid app's name
        appName:'sandbox',
      });
```

```
      // STEP 2: retrieve a list of books from the server
      $(document).ready(function () {
        refreshFeed();

        function refreshFeed() {
          // a new Collection object that will
          // be used to hold the full feed list
          var my_books = new Usergrid.Collection(
                            {"client":apigee, "type":"books"});

          //make sure messages are pulled back in order
          my_books.fetch(
            // Success Callback
            function(){
              // STEP 3: create a list with book details
              var html = "";
              while(my_books.hasNextEntity()) {
                var current_book = my_books.getNextEntity();

                html += '<li>';
                html += '<h3>' + current_book.get('title') +'</h3>';
                html += '<p>'+ current_book.get('author') +'</p>';
                html += '</li>';
              }

              // STEP 4: render the book details
              $("#messages-list").html(html);

              // STEP 5: render the book details
              $('#messages-list').listview('refresh');
            },

            // Failure Callback
            function(){
              $("#messages-list")
                .html("<li>Error retrieving the book list</li>");
            }
          );
        }
      });
    </script>
</head>

<body>
    <div data-role="page" data-theme="c" id="page-messages-list">
      <div data-role="header" data-theme="b">
        <h1>My Books</h1>
        <a href="#page-new-message" id="btn-compose"
           data-icon="plus" data-iconpos="right" data-inline="true"
           data-role="button" data-rel="dialog" data-transition="fade"
           class="ui-btn-right">Compose</a>
      </div>

      <ul id="messages-list" data-role="listview" data-inset="true" >
        <li>No messages here!</li>
      </ul>
    </div>
```

```
<div data-role="page" data-theme="b" id="page-new-message">
  <div data-role="header" data-theme="b">
    <h1>Add a New Book</h1>
  </div>

  <div data-role="content">
    <form>
      <label for="content">Title</label>
      <textarea id="content" class="input-xlarge" rows="3"
        style="margin: 0px; width: 100%; height: 125px;">
      </textarea>

      <label for="content2">Author</label>
      <textarea id="content2" class="input-xlarge" rows="3"
        style="margin: 0px; width: 100%; height: 125px;">
      </textarea>
    </form>

    <a href="#page-messages-list" id="btn-close-new-message"
      data-role="button" data-theme="c"
      data-inline="true">Cancel</a>
    <button id="post-message" data-inline="true">Post</button>

<script>
  $("#post-message").on("click", function() {
    // get form values for new book:
    var title  = $("#content").val();
    var author = $("#content2").val();

    options = {"type": "books",
               "title": title,
               "author": author};

    apigee.createEntity(options, function(err, response) {
      if (err) { alert("write failed");
      } else { alert("write succeeded"); }
    });
  });
</script>
  </div>
  </div>
 </body>
</html>
```

Listing 10.1 contains six main sections of JavaScript code that perform different functionality. Step 1 sets the user-specific details of the user account on Apigee:

```
var apigee = new Usergrid.Client({
      orgName:'oswald',
      appName:'sandbox',
});
```

Keep in mind that the data in the preceding account is in the Apigee "sandbox," which means that the data is subject to change, and therefore your results may vary from what you see presented in this chapter.

Step 2 retrieves the book-related data from the Apigee server with this code snippet:

```
var my_books = new Usergrid.Collection(
                    {"client":apigee, "type":"books" });
```

Step 3 contains a loop that iterates through the variable my_books in order to extract the information for each book, as shown here:

```
var html = "";
while(my_books.hasNextEntity()) {
  var current_book = my_books.getNextEntity();

  html += '<li>';
  html += '<h3>' + current_book.get('title') +'</h3>';
  html += '<p>'+ current_book.get('author') +'</p>';
  html += '</li>';
}
```

Step 4 updates the list of books with this code snippet:

```
$("#messages-list").html(html);
```

Step 5 updates the screen with the newly constructed list of books with this code snippet:

```
$('#messages-list').listview('refresh');
```

The failure callback is a JavaScript function that updates the <ul> element with an error message.

The <body> element contains jQuery Mobile code that is familiar to you from Chapter 9. Notice the final block of code in a <script> tag that extracts the content of the input fields for the title and author of a new book (supplied by users). A JSON object called options is created that contains the values of title and author, after which an Apigee API is invoked in order to save the new book on the server. An appropriate message is displayed depending on whether the API invocation succeeded or failed. The entire <script> code block is reproduced here:

```
<script>
    $("#post-message").on("click", function() {
        // get form values for new book:
        var title  = $("#content").val();
        var author = $("#content2").val();

        options = {"type": "books",
                   "title": title,
                   "author": author};

        apigee.createEntity(options, function(err, response) {
            if (err) { alert("write failed");
            } else { alert("write succeeded"); }
        });
    });
</script>
```

The next section requires some context: the purpose of learning how to render a 3D bar chart in HTML5 `Canvas` is to enable you to follow the code sample in the final section of this chapter. The final section contains an example of retrieving data from an HTML5 Web Socket server and then rendering that data in a bar chart using HTML5 `Canvas`.

RENDERING 3D BAR CHARTS

One of the appendices for this book discusses HTML5 `Canvas` and provides examples of rendering 2D shapes in HTML5 `Canvas`. You can skim through that Appendix if you need to familiarize yourself with the APIs that are used in Listing 10.2.

In this section, you will see how to render a set of cube-like shapes, each of which consists of a top face (a parallelogram), a front face (a rectangle), and a right face (a parallelogram). Consequently, you can use basic APIs in order to render a cube in HTML5 `Canvas`.

The HTML page `BarChart13D1.html` in Listing 10.2 illustrates how to render a 3D bar chart with a three-dimensional effect in HTML5 `Canvas`.

LISTING 10.2 BarChart13D1.html

```
<!DOCTYPE html>
<html lang="en">
<head>
  <meta charset="utf-8" />
  <title>HTML5 Canvas 3D Bar Chart Linear Gradient</title>

  <script>
    var currentX    = 0;
    var currentY    = 0;
    var barCount    = 12;
    var barWidth    = 40;
    var barHeight   = 0;
    var maxHeight   = 330;
    var slantX      = barWidth/3;
    var slantY      = barWidth/3;
    var shadowX     = 2;
    var shadowY     = 2;
    var axisFontSize = 12;
    var fontSize    = 16;
    var labelY      = 0;
    var indentY     = 10;
    var leftBorder  = 30;
    var topBorder   = 15;
    var arrowWidth  = 10;
    var arrowHeight = 6;
    var topShading  = "#888";
    var rightShading = "#444";
    var xAxisWidth  = (barCount+1)*barWidth;
    var yAxisHeight = maxHeight;
    var barHeights  = new Array(barCount);
    var elem, context, gradient1;
```

```
function drawGraph() {
   elem = document.getElementById('myCanvas');
   if (!elem || !elem.getContext) {
     return;
   }

   // Get the canvas 2d context.
   context = elem.getContext('2d');
   if (!context) {
     return;
   }

   drawBarChart();
}

function drawAndLabelAxes() {
   // code omitted for brevity
}

function randomBarValues() {
   for(var i=0; i<barCount; i++) {
      barHeight = (maxHeight-indentY)*Math.random();
      barHeights[i] = barHeight;
   }
}

function drawBarChart() {
   // clear the canvas before drawing new set of rectangles
   context.clearRect(0, 0, elem.width, elem.height);

   drawAndLabelAxes();
   randomBarValues();
   drawElements();
}

function drawElements() {
   for(var i=0; i<barCount; i++) {
      currentX = leftBorder+i*barWidth;
      currentY = maxHeight-barHeights[i];

      // front face (rectangle)
      gradient1 = context.createLinearGradient(
                           currentX,
                           currentY,
                           currentX+barWidth,
                           currentY+barHeights[i]);

      gradient1.addColorStop(0,   '#f00');
      gradient1.addColorStop(0.3,'#000');
      gradient1.addColorStop(0.6,'#ff0');
      gradient1.addColorStop(1,   '#00f');

      context.fillStyle = gradient1;

      context.shadowColor   = "rgba(100,100,100,.5)";
      context.shadowOffsetX = 3;
```

```
         context.shadowOffsetY = 3;
         context.shadowBlur    = 5;

         context.fillRect(currentX,
                          currentY,
                          barWidth,
                          barHeights[i]);

         // top face (parallelogram)
         // CCW from lower-left vertex
         context.beginPath();
         context.fillStyle = topShading;
         context.shadowColor   = "rgba(100,100,100,.5)";
         context.shadowOffsetX = 3;
         context.shadowOffsetY = 3;
         context.shadowBlur    = 5;

         context.moveTo(currentX, currentY);
         context.lineTo(currentX+barWidth, currentY);
         context.lineTo(currentX+barWidth+slantX,
                        currentY-slantY);
         context.lineTo(currentX+slantX,
                        currentY-slantY);
         context.closePath();
         context.fill();

         // right face (parallelogram)
         // CW from upper-left vertex
         context.beginPath();
         context.fillStyle = rightShading;

         context.shadowColor   = "rgba(100,100,100,.5)";
         context.shadowOffsetX = 3;
         context.shadowOffsetY = 3;
         context.shadowBlur    = 5;

         context.moveTo(currentX+barWidth, currentY);
         context.lineTo(currentX+barWidth+slantX,
                        currentY-slantY);
         context.lineTo(currentX+barWidth+slantX,
                        currentY+barHeights[i]-slantY);
         context.lineTo(currentX+barWidth,
                        currentY+barHeights[i]);
         context.closePath();
         context.fill();
      }

      drawBarText();
   }

   function drawBarText() {
      // Define some drawing attributes
      context.font = "bold "+fontSize+"pt New Times Roman";
      context.lineWidth   = 2;
      context.strokeStyle = "#000";
```

```
        for(var i=0; i<barCount; i++) {
           context.beginPath();
           currentX = leftBorder+i*barWidth;
           currentY = maxHeight-barHeights[i]+fontSize/4;
         //context.fillStyle = fillColors[i%4];
           context.fillStyle = "#000";

           barHeight = Math.floor(barHeights[i]);

           // Outline a text string
           context.strokeText(""+barHeight,
                              currentX+shadowX,
                              currentY+shadowY);

           // Fill a text string
           context.fillStyle = "#F00";
           context.fillText(""+barHeight,
                            currentX,
                            currentY);
        }
     }
   </script>

   <style type="text/css">
     canvas {
        border: 5px solid #888;
        background: #CCC;
     }
   </style>
</head>

<body onload="drawGraph();">
   <header>
     <h1>HTML5 Canvas 3D Bar Chart</h1>
   </header>

   <figure>
    <canvas id="myCanvas" width="600" height="350">No support for
Canvas</canvas>
   </figure>

   <input type="button" onclick="drawGraph();return false"
          value="Update Graph Values" />
</body>
</html>
```

Listing 10.2 adds two parallelograms to each bar element of the bar chart: one is above the bar element (which is a rectangle) and one is to the right of the bar element, thereby creating a three-dimensional effect. The main loop in Listing 10.2 creates a linear gradient (with four stop colors) that is used for rendering the top, front, and right face of each bar element in the bar chart.

Figure 10.1 displays a three-dimensional bar chart in which the height of individual bar elements are randomly generated numbers (scaled to fit the

HTML5 Canvas 3D Bar Chart

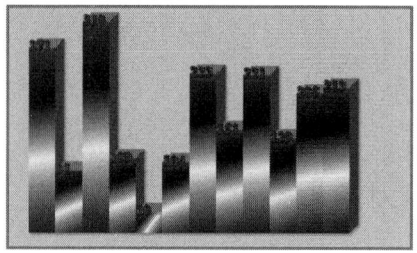

FIGURE 10.1 A 3D Bar Chart in a Chrome
Browser on a Macbook Pro.

screen). Whenever users click on the button with the label "Update Graph
Values," the bar chart is displayed with a new set of random numbers.

UPDATING HTML5 CANVAS BAR CHARTS WITH A WEBSOCKET SERVER

The previous section showed you how to use jQuery Mobile so that you
can display a bar chart on a mobile device. In this section, you will learn
how to dynamically update and render a bar chart on a client browser with
data that is periodically "pushed" from a WebSocket server. Admittedly this
book does not provide a thorough explanation of HTML5 Web Sockets, so
you might find it necessary to read an article (perform an Internet search)
to give you some background information about HTML5 Web Sockets.
Fortunately, the WebSocket code in this example is straightforward and
consolidated in one JavaScript function called `getWebSocketData()` in
Listing 10.3.

The code sample in this section consists of three files: the HTML5 Web
page `JQWSBarChart1.html`, for rendering the bar chart, the Python script
`echo_wsh.py` (using Python 2.7.1) that sends data to the client browser, and
the shell script `run.sh` that launches the WebSocket server.

Listing 10.3 displays a portion of the contents of `JQWSBarChart1.
html` that illustrates how to receive data from a WebSocket server and re-
fresh a bar chart with that data in HTML5 `Canvas`. Note that the code for
the bar chart has been omitted for brevity, but the complete listing is available
on the DVD.

LISTING 10.3 JQWSBarChart1.html

```
<!DOCTYPE HTML>
<html lang="en">
<head>
  <meta charset="utf-8" />
  <title>WebSockets and Bar Chart</title>
  <link href="CSS32Background1.css"
        rel="stylesheet" type="text/css">
```

```
<script
  src="http://code.jquery.com/jquery-2.0.0b1.js">
</script>

<script
  src="http://code.jquery.com/jquery-migrate-1.1.0.js">
</script>

<script>
  var currentX      = 0;
  var currentY      = 0;
  var barCount      = 10;
  var barWidth      = 40;
  var barHeight     = 0;
  var maxHeight     = 300;
  var xAxisWidth    = (2*barCount+1)*barWidth/2;
  var yAxisHeight   = maxHeight;
  var labelY        = 0;
  var indentY       = 5;
  var shadowX       = 2;
  var shadowY       = 2;
  var axisFontSize = 12;
  var fontSize      = 16;
  var leftBorder    = 50;
  var topBorder     = 50;
  var arrowWidth    = 10;
  var arrowHeight   = 6;
  var barHeights    = new Array(barCount);
  var fillColors    = ['#f00', '#0f0', '#ff0', '#00f'];
  var elem, context, gradient1;

  var WSData = "", sendMsg = "Client-side Message", receiveMsg = "";
  var theTimeout, pollingDelay = 2000;

  function initialGraph() {
    var foundCanvas = setup();

    if(foundCanvas == true) {
      getWebSocketData();
    }
  }

  function setup() {
    // Get the canvas element
    elem = document.getElementById('myCanvas');
    if(!elem || !elem.getContext) {
      return false;
    }

    // Get the canvas 2d context
    context = elem.getContext('2d');
    if(!context) {
      return false;
    }

    return true;
  }
```

```
///// bar chart code omitted for brevity

function getWebSocketData() {
  if ("WebSocket" in window) {
    console.log("Your Browser supports WebSockets");

    // Open a web socket
    var ws = new WebSocket("ws://localhost:9998/echo");

    // specify handlers for open/close/message/error
    ws.onopen = function() {
      // Web Socket is connected: send data using send()
      ws.send(sendMsg);
      console.log("Sending Message to server: "+sendMsg);
    };

    ws.onmessage = function (evt) {
      var receivedMsg = evt.data;
      console.log("Message from server: "+receivedMsg);
      setupBarChart(receivedMsg);
    };

    ws.onclose = function() {
      // websocket is closed.
      console.log("Connection is closed...");
    };

    ws.onerror = function(evt) {
      console.log("Error occurred: "+evt.data);
    };
  } else {
    // The browser doesn't support WebSocket
    console.log("WebSocket NOT supported by your Browser!");
  }
}

function setupBarChart(dataStr) {
  // populate the barHeights array
  barHeights = dataStr.split(" ");

  barCount   = barHeights.length;

  drawGraph2();
}
</script>
</head>

<body onload="initialGraph();">
  <script>
    $(document).ready(function() {
      $("#StartClientPoll").click(function() {
        getWebSocketData();
        theTimeout = setInterval("getWebSocketData()", pollingDelay);
      })
```

```
      $("#StopClientPoll").click(function() {
         clearInterval(theTimeout);
         theTimeout = null;
      })

      $("#StartWSPull").click(function() {
         getWebSocketData();
         theTimeout = setInterval("getWebSocketData()", pollingDelay);
      })

      $("#StopWSPull").click(function() {
         clearInterval(theTimeout);
         theTimeout = null;
      })
   });
</script>

<div id="conn"></div>

<div>
   <canvas id="myCanvas" width="800" height="400">No support for
Canvas
            alt="Example rendering of a bar chart">
   </canvas>
</div>

<div id="WSDataDiv">
   <input type="button" id="StartClientPoll"
          value="Start Client Polling" />
   <input type="button" id="StopClientPoll"
          value="Stop Client Polling" />
   <input type="button" id="StartWSPull"
          value="Start Server" />
   <input type="button" id="StopWSPull"
          value="Stop Server" />
</div>
</body>
</html>
```

One point to keep in mind is that some other browsers may implement older versions of the WebSockets protocol. In this example, Chrome 19 implements the current WebSockets protocol that is available in late 2012.

The <body> element in Listing 10.3 invokes the function initial-Graph() that performs some initialization and then invokes the function getWebSocketData() to get the bar chart data (if the HTML5 <canvas> element exists in the Web page), as shown here:

```
function initialGraph() {
   var foundCanvas = setup();

   if(foundCanvas == true) {
      getWebSocketData();
   }
}
```

Next, the function `getWebSocketData()` implements the standard callback functions in JavaScript, including the `onmessage` function, which gets the data from the WebSocket server passes the data to the `setupBarChart()` function for rendering the bar chart, as shown here:

```
function getWebSocketData() {
  if ("WebSocket" in window) {
    // Open a web socket
    var ws = new WebSocket("ws://localhost:9998/echo");

    // code omitted for brevity
    ws.onmessage = function (evt) {
        var receivedMsg = evt.data;
        console.log("Message from server: "+receivedMsg);
        setupBarChart(receivedMsg);
      };
}
```

As you know, the code samples in this book render correctly in `WebKit`-based browsers, and in some cases the code samples work in other browsers. One exception is the code snippet shown in bold in the previous code block, which will not work in most versions of Firefox; however, it's possible that future versions of Firefox will support this code.

The `setupBarChart()` JavaScript function accepts a string parameter that consists of a space-delimited set of values for the bar heights of the bar chart, which is used to populate a JavaScript array with those bar heights, as shown here:

```
function setupBarChart(dataStr) {
    // populate the barHeights array
    barHeights = dataStr.split(" ");

    barCount   = barHeights.length;

    drawGraph2();
}
```

The rendering of the bar chart is handled by the JavaScript function `drawGraph2()`, which is not shown in Listing 10.3.

The other part to consider is the code on the WebSocket server that returns the data values for the bar chart. The data is retrieved with the following code snippet that is contained in the `getWebSocketData()` function, as shown here:

```
// Open a web socket
var ws = new WebSocket("ws://localhost:9998/echo");
```

Now let's turn our attention to the server-side code. Before delving into the details of the code, you need to download `pywebsocket`, which is here:

https://code.google.com/p/pywebsocket/

Now let's examine the relevant portion of the Python script `echo_wsh`.
`py` that sends data from the WebSockets server to the client (via port `9998`),
whose contents are displayed in Listing 10.4.

LISTING 10.4 echo_wsh.py

```
# Copyright 2011, Google Inc.
# All rights reserved.
#
# Redistribution and use in source and binary forms, with or
without
# modification, are permitted provided that the following
conditions are
# met:
#
#     * Redistributions of source code must retain the above
copyright
# notice, this list of conditions and the following disclaimer.
#     * Redistributions in binary form must reproduce the above
# copyright notice, this list of conditions and the following
disclaimer
# in the documentation and/or other materials provided with the
# distribution.
#     * Neither the name of Google Inc. nor the names of its
# contributors may be used to endorse or promote products derived
from
# this software without specific prior written permission.
#
# THIS SOFTWARE IS PROVIDED BY THE COPYRIGHT HOLDERS AND
CONTRIBUTORS
# "AS IS" AND ANY EXPRESS OR IMPLIED WARRANTIES, INCLUDING, BUT
NOT
# LIMITED TO, THE IMPLIED WARRANTIES OF MERCHANTABILITY AND
FITNESS FOR
# A PARTICULAR PURPOSE ARE DISCLAIMED. IN NO EVENT SHALL THE
COPYRIGHT
# OWNER OR CONTRIBUTORS BE LIABLE FOR ANY DIRECT, INDIRECT,
INCIDENTAL,
# SPECIAL, EXEMPLARY, OR CONSEQUENTIAL DAMAGES (INCLUDING, BUT NOT
# LIMITED TO, PROCUREMENT OF SUBSTITUTE GOODS OR SERVICES; LOSS OF
USE,
# DATA, OR PROFITS; OR BUSINESS INTERRUPTION) HOWEVER CAUSED AND
ON ANY
# THEORY OF LIABILITY, WHETHER IN CONTRACT, STRICT LIABILITY, OR
TORT
# (INCLUDING NEGLIGENCE OR OTHERWISE) ARISING IN ANY WAY OUT OF
THE USE
# OF THIS SOFTWARE, EVEN IF ADVISED OF THE POSSIBILITY OF SUCH
DAMAGE.

_GOODBYE_MESSAGE = u'Goodbye'

from random import randint

def web_socket_do_extra_handshake(request):
    pass  # Always accept.
```

```
def web_socket_transfer_data(request):
    while True:
        line = request.ws_stream.receive_message()
        if line is None:
            return
        if isinstance(line, unicode):
            barCount = 10;
            randomValues = ""

            for x in range(1, barCount):
                randomValues = randomValues + str(randint(50, 300))+" "

            print 'randomValues2: %s' % randomValues
            request.ws_stream.send_message(randomValues,
                                binary=False)

            if line == _GOODBYE_MESSAGE:
                return
        else:
            print 'Sending2: %s' % line
            request.ws_stream.send_message(line, binary=True)
```

The cold shown in bold in Listing 10.4 is the code that creates a string containing a randomly generated set of integers that represent the ten bar heights of a bar chart:

```
barCount = 10;
randomValues = ""

for x in range(1, barCount):
    randomValues = randomValues + str(randint(50, 300))+" "

    print 'randomValues2: %s' % randomValues
```

After the string of concatenated bar heights has been created, it is sent to the client with the following code snippet:

```
request.ws_stream.send_message(randomValues, binary=False)
```

The third file that we need is a simple Bourne shell script `run.sh` that launches the WebSocket server on port 9998.

LISTING 10.5 run.sh

```
CURRDIR=`pwd`
PYTHONPATH=$CURRDIR
python ./mod_pywebsocket/standalone.py -p 9998 -d $CURRDIR/example
```

Listing 10.5 is straightforward: it sets two shell script variables and then launches the Python script `standalone.py` located in the `mod_pywebsocket` subdirectory, specifying port `9998` and also the `example` subdirectory of `$CURRDIR`, which is the parent directory of the Python script `echo_wsh.py` in Listing 10.4.

Open a command shell, navigate to the subdirectory `pywebsocket/src`, and launch the shell script in Listing 10.5 as follows:

```
./run.sh
```

Listing 10.4 contains a copyright notice that is required for displaying the contents of this Python script. The new section of code (displayed in bold in Listing 10.4), is shown here:

```
barCount = 10;
randomValues = ""

for x in range(1, barCount):
  randomValues = randomValues + str(randint(50, 300))+" "

request.ws_stream.send_message(randomValues, binary=False)
```

Figure 10.2 displays a very colorful bar chart and also the data that is returned from a server, which specifies the height of each bar element in the graph.

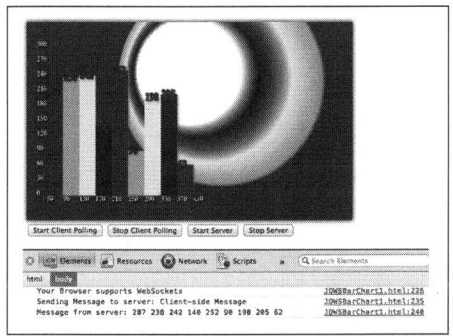

FIGURE 10.2 A Bar Chart Using HTML5 WebSockets.

If you prefer using open source toolkits for handling the various WebSocket details for multiple browsers, there are also jQuery plugins available that use jQuery as a layer of abstraction on top of WebSockets (support for multiple browsers), such as the one that is here:

https://code.google.com/p/jquery-graceful-websocket/

This jQuery plugin provides fallback support for Ajax if WebSockets is unavailable, along with options to override the default options.

SUMMARY

This chapter showed you how to create hybrid HTML5 mobile applications that perform various types of Internet access. The first example used a combination of jQuery and Apigee APIs to retrieve and also post JSON-based data on a remote server. Next you learned how to create a 3D bar chart with gradient effects in HTML5 `Canvas`. Finally, you learned how to retrieve data from an HTML5 Web Socket server and then render that data in a bar chart.

ON THE DVD

T he DVD contains an assortment of code samples, appendices, and videos that accompany the material in the book.

CODE SAMPLES

The HTML5 Web page `DragDrop1.html` shows you how to handle Drag-and-Drop functionality in "pure" JavaScript, and the Web page `JQ-Geolocation1.html` shows you how to use the geoPlugin (which is not a jQuery plugin) for Geolocation.

- The HTML5 Web pages `Skew1.html` and the CSS stylesheet `Skew1.css` illustrate how to create skew effects.
- The HTML5 Web page `JQMNestedListViews1.html` is a jQuery Mobile Web page that illustrates how to render nested lists and how to navigate between pages when users click on list items.
- The HTML5 Web page `JQMMenu1.html` illustrates how to create a sliding menu.
- The HTML Web page `JQFileInfo1.html` illustrates how to use jQuery in order to display the attributes of a file that is selected by users.
- The DVD also contains the Android application `ThreeDCube1.apk` that you can deploy to any Android device that supports Android 4.x (including Google Glass).

VIDEOS

The DVD contains the following HTML5-related videos:

- HTML5Intro.mov (Introduction to HTML5)
- HTML5Audio1.mov (HTML5 and the <audio> tag)
- HTML5Video1.mov (HTML5 and a <video> tag)
- HTML5SemanticMarkup.mov (HTML5 and Semantic Markup)

The DVD also contains the following CSS3-related videos:

- CSS3Introduction.mov (introduction to CSS3)
- CSS3LinearGradients1.mov (CSS3 and Linear Gradients)
- CSS3RadialGradient1.mov (CSS3 and Radial Gradients)

APPENDICES

The DVD contains appendices for the following topics:

- jQuery Concepts
- Introduction to Android

INDEX